MOB RULE

Unmasking the Radical Leftists at Our Doorsteps

JAKE JACOBS, PH.D.

FREILING
PUBLISHING

Published by Freiling Publishing, a division of Freiling Agency, LLC.

P.O. Box 1264,
Warrenton, VA 20188

www.FreilingPublishing.com

ISBN 978-1-950948-38-3

Printed in the United States of America

"Dr. Jacobs exposes the dark underpinnings of the Marxist upheaval swamping our communities and shines a floodlight on the Radical Left's tactics in their war on religious liberty. Mob Rule is a clarion call for conservatives that delivers the intellectual firepower to repel the infiltration of anti-American ideology festering among our country's youth and institutions."

—Wisconsin State Senator André Jacque
(R- De Pere)

"As a lifelong educator, Dr. Jacobs is at the forefront of this coming conflict. Our educational system has been hijacked, and Marxist violence is here... As a Navy Seal Warrant Officer with 27 years in the teams, I have seen combat. Mob Rule is an insightful, sobering account of what our new "front lines" look like. Dr. Jake, thank you for the wakeup call...we must regain control of our education system now!"

—Bobby Richardson

Dedicated to the great 1776-American freedom fighters: William Lee, Frederick Douglass, William Carney, Harriet Jacobs, Doris Miller, Joe Jacobs, the Tuskegee Airmen, Rosa Parks, and Martin Luther King Jr.

Contents

Introduction **The Road to Hell Is Paved with Good Intentions** 1

Chapter 1 **Leftism: Antifa and Black Lives Matter** 9

Chapter 2 **Black Lives Matter and Marxism** 35

Chapter 3 **Uncle Tom: Lies, Damned Lies, and Statistics** 73

Chapter 4 **Socialism, Symbolism, and Statues** 109

Chapter 5 **Frederick Douglass' "4th of July" Speech and Zinn's Sins** 127

Chapter 6 **1619 Project versus July 4, 1776** .. 141

Chapter 7 **1776 American History in Black and White** 159

Chapter 8 **They Were There in 1776!** 187

Bibliography 197

Introduction

"The road to hell is paved with good intentions" was supposedly coined by the great English poet, playwright, and moralist Samuel Johnson in 1775. He borrowed this phrase from St. Bernard of Clairvaux (1091–1115), who declared, "Hell is full of good intentions or desires." Throughout the history of Western civilization, we see individuals who intended to achieve good in society but were used by ruthless and immoral Machiavellians for their diabolical ends.

In reality, in America and the world today, the lefty-revolutionary road to hell is paved with BAD intentions. It is a road of serfdom, a road of slavery to the state, and a road to perdition that leads to *"mobocracy"* or "mob rule." This brings the destruction of life, liberty, and democracy as we've known and experienced in the United States and other liberal democracies for over two centuries.

Who are the main actors in this tragedy of evil intentions? They are sundry leftists from Antifa and Black Lives Matter to the Democratic Socialists of America. Sadly, many of them are members of the world's oldest active political party, the party of my parents and grandparents: the Democratic Party of the United States of America.

History is full of tragic deaths and shots heard around the world that in a split second can change the destiny of a country and of the world forever. The classic "shot heard round the world" was, of course, on April 19th, 1775, at the Battle of Concord. This was when patriotic minutemen fired shots at the British troops, starting the American Revolution and leading to the birth of the United States of America and our wonderful republic under God in 1776.

Another classic "shot heard round the world" was on June 28, 1914, when anarchist-communist Gavrilo Princip assassinated Archduke Franz Ferdinand and his wife Sophie of Austria. Princip's bullets were the sparks that led to the flames of World War I and the death of tens of millions of people.

The latest "death heard round the world" occurred on May 25, 2020, when a Minneapolis police officer, Derek Chauvin, arrested George Floyd, who was intoxicated with drugs and had attempted to buy cigarettes with a counterfeit $20 bill. Within a matter of a few minutes, Officer Chauvin, who is white, had George Floyd, who was black, pinned to the ground. While Floyd pleaded that he could not breathe, Chauvin kept his knee on Floyd's neck for nearly nine minutes. Floyd died in the process. The negligent arrest by Officer Chauvin and the three assisting officers was the spark that led to the flames of demonstrations, protests, and riots that exploded in more than 400 cities in the U.S. and around the world. During the protests, over 30 people were killed, both black and white and many colors in between. Thousands of homes and businesses were seriously damaged and destroyed, costing into the billions of dollars.

The tragic death of George Floyd and the subsequent protests and riots that followed occurred in the midst of a so-called global pandemic—the crisis of COVID-19—a Chinese virus that saw governments shut down major parts of the world, with serious political ramifications of government control, dictates, and mandates.

Magically and in an instant, government quarantine policies and social distancing rules were no longer heeded as thousands of citizens flocked to the streets in a fistful of rage over George Floyd's death. Cries of "Systemic racism!" "Institutional racism!" "Genocide!" "White supremacy!" "Kill the cops!" "No justice, no peace!" and "Trump is a Nazi!" filled the bloodied streets of America. Over 1,000 police officers of many diverse backgrounds were seriously hurt. Some were murdered. While the name of George Floyd was ubiquitous with the lefty media, Antifa, and Black Lives Matter (BLM), there was little to no mention of 77-year-old retired black American police captain David Dorn, who was shot during the George Floyd riots by 24-year-old black American Stephen Cannon.

Most government officials—the overwhelming majority of them Democratic mayors, police chiefs, and governors—and the activist media readily invoked George Floyd's name, but very few mentioned David Dorn. These same officials, who were very adamant on May 24 about strict quarantine and social distancing policies, looked the other way or participated in the demonstrations as quarantine social-distancing violations exploded exponentially.

The juxtaposition of the COVID-19 Chinese virus crisis— with Communist China playing a notoriously diabolical role on the world stage—with the George Floyd crisis created a cacophony of conflicting narratives. The Communist Chinese on one hand and the rhetoric and actions by the mostly Democratic government officials on the other hand filled the mind with questions of what was ultimately behind the many violent actions of the Floyd demonstrators and the reactions of Democratic politicians and government officials.

What was behind these multifaceted actions? Good or bad intentions? Could it be both? This is what *MOB-RULE* is all about.

On June 1, 2020, U.S. President Donald Trump, speaking from the Rose Garden, issued a statement titled "Law & Justice" in which he declared:

> All Americans were rightly sickened and revolted by the brutal death of George Floyd. My administration is fully committed that, for George and his family, justice will be served. He will not have died in vain. But we cannot allow the righteous cries and peaceful protesters to be drowned out by an angry mob. The biggest victims of the rioting are peace-loving citizens in our poorest communities, and as their President, I will fight to keep them safe. I will fight to protect you. I am your President of law and order, and an ally of all peaceful protesters.
>
> But in recent days, our nation has been gripped by professional anarchists, violent mobs, arsonists, looters, criminals, rioters, Antifa, and others. A number of state and local governments have failed to take necessary action to safeguard their residents. Innocent people have been savagely beaten, like the young man in Dallas, Texas, who was left dying on the street, or the woman in

Upstate New York viciously attacked by dangerous thugs.

Small-business owners have seen their dreams utterly destroyed. New York's Finest have been hit in the face with bricks. Brave nurses, who have battled the virus, are afraid to leave their homes. A police precinct station has been overrun. Here in the nation's capital, the Lincoln Memorial and the World War Two Memorial have been vandalized. One of our most historic churches was set ablaze. A federal officer in California, an African American enforcement hero, was shot and killed.

These are not acts of peaceful protest. These are acts of domestic terror. The destruction of innocent life and the spilling of innocent blood is an offense to humanity and a crime against God.

America needs creation, not destruction; cooperation, not contempt; security, not anarchy; healing, not hatred; justice, not chaos.

Notice the president's commitment to protect "all peaceful protestors ... righteous cries ... who should not be 'drowned out by an angry mob.'" He goes on to describe the "angry mob" as "professional anarchists, violent mobs, arsonists, looters, criminals, rioters, Antifa, and others." While this book will cover the so-called "righteous cries of the peaceful protestors," we will deal in detail with the "angry mob," which I call *"mobocrats"* in their multifarious form. *"Mobocrat"* is a portmanteau of democrat, bureaucrat, and mob. I first encountered the *mobocrats* in Madison, Wisconsin, in 2011, while defending Republican Governor

Scott Walker. The *mobocrats* swarmed down to our state capital, Madison, Wisconsin, and violently took over our beautiful Capitol while declaring that Governor Walker and Republicans were Nazis, fascists, racists, etc.

In my 2012 book *Mobocracy*, I dealt with the political left's cultural and political war to destroy our republic under God. The backdrop to *Mobocracy* was the attempt by Democrats and leftists to destroy Wisconsin Governor Scott Walker's attempt to balance our state budget and stop the public school unions from monopolizing taxpayers' money for their Democratic political gain and control.

As Democrats joined in force with anarchists, socialists, communists, and many other hardcore lefty organizations, they declared that Governor Scott Walker and his conservative, libertarian, and Republican supporters were Hitler, Stalin, Mussolini, Nazis, and Fascists. Wonderfully, the citizens of Wisconsin rose up to the smear campaign and resoundingly destroyed their lefty "Recall Revolution" and voted for Governor Scott Walker in even larger numbers than the first time, re-electing him and making American history in the process.

So what was it that caused such an affinity between Democrats and a hodgepodge of various political left-wing expressions? Not all Democrats were calling Governor Walker "Hitler" and his supporters "Nazis" or "fascists"; many of them simply felt Governor Walker was unjustly taking away a part of their hard-earned income. While I disagreed with my Democrat teaching colleagues, I defended their right to peaceably protest. Sadly, a profound element of militancy and hate-filled Democratic ranks transformed a significant number of them into *mobocrats*. That's when, in 2011, I realized that the party I was a card-carrying member of (I voted for Jimmy Carter in 1976) and the party of my parents and grandparents (my mother loved telling the story of my grandfather, a farmer, crying by his tractor when she told him FDR died in 1945) was gradually being taken over by hardcore lefty ideologues and *mobocrats*.

Today it is no longer gradual. It is exponential. The Democratic Party and the DNC have been taken over by hardcore leftism and the *mobocrats*, and sadly, the great liberal Democrats of years gone by are no longer. *Mobocrats* drive the agenda as Democratic leaders nationwide kowtow to their politically correct demands. From socialist Alexandria Ocasio-Cortez; radical Muslims Rashida Talib and Ilhan Omar; to Marxists Colin Kaepernick and BLM founders Alicia Garza, Opal Tometi, and Patrisse Cullors, the radical-lefty tail now wags the Democratic dog.

Gone are the Martin Luther King Jrs., Harry S Trumans, Daniel Patrick Moynihans, Hubert Humphreys, and the Kennedy brothers that my parents, grandparents, and I admired. There is a new breed of left-wing Democrat-*mobocrat* who has on a leash the old guard of Joe Biden, Nancy Pelosi, Jerry Nadler, and Chuck Schumer. These *mobocrats* are nasty and hell-bent to spread their leftist revolution in America. Their disinformation, misinformation, revisionist history, and indoctrination in our government schools must be exposed for what they are: lies upon lies upon lies. These lefty lies feed the flames of the lefty revolution that plagued our cities and our nation during the summer and fall of 2020 and beyond.

You'll notice I have already used the terms "left-wing," "lefty," and "leftists" in contradistinction to life, liberty, and liberal democracy. Words do have meanings that convey ideas, and we all know ideas have consequences. To understand how the *mobocrats* have infiltrated American society from top to bottom, let us begin by understanding what leftism, Antifa, and BLM (Black Lives Matter) are all about.

Chapter 1

Leftism: Antifa and Black Lives Matter

"Leftism seeks to undo most of values that are distinct to Judeo-Christian religion."
(Dennis Prager)

One could argue that "leftism" was born the day the arrogant tyrant King Nimrod commanded the people to build a tower to the heavens in a futile attempt to defy YAHWEH-God, the God of Israel, the God of the Judeo-Christian tradition. The Jewish historian Flavious Josephus in his *Antiquities of the Jews* tells us:

> Now it was Nimrod who excited them to such an affront and contempt of God. He was the grandson of Ham, the son of Noah, a bold man, and of great strength of hand. He persuaded them not to ascribe it to God as if it were through his means they were happy, but to believe that it was their own courage which procured that happiness. He also gradually changed the government into

tyranny, seeing no other way of turning men from the fear of God, but to bring them into a constant dependence on his power.

This biblical story from the book of Genesis 11:1–9 exposes the sinful hubristic act of defiance against the creator of the universe, YAHWEH-God, in which the king replaces God with government dependency to make his subjects "happy."

"Happiness" has driven many people throughout the ages to embrace the philosophy that will create a utopia or heaven on earth without God.

Leftism's worldview was shaped during the French Revolution when they called for the overthrow of the established order of monarchy and Christianity. Even the term "left-wing" derives from the radicals of the French Revolution. In the name of "reason," a number of "enlightened" thinkers, citing the works of Voltaire and Rousseau, declared that mankind's problems were not internal due to the corruption of the human heart and the human condition of sin as expressed by Judaism and Christianity, but the problems were "societal," outside of man, due to the oppression of corrupt rulers within the state and Christianity.

Jacque Hebert, Antoinie-Francois Momoro, Pierre Gaspard Chamette, Joseph Fouche, and the notorious "King" of the Bloody Reign of Terror Maximilien Robespierre called for the "de-Christianization of France" and the establishment of a "Cult of Reason." Man's mind and nature would be worshipped so as to perfect man and society with a "new man" dedicated to "one God only, *le peuple*," or "the people," and their new god: The STATE.

French Revolutionary orators such as Georges Danton warned that this Cult of Reason's declaration for the "de-Christianization" of French society would create chaos and blood in the streets. This utopian cult of reason did just that as the streets of Paris and many major cities throughout France experienced the infamous "Bloody Reign of Terror," in which hundreds of thousands were guillotined and slaughtered by planned execution and the *mobocrats* of the day.

While Robespierre may have been a guillotined victim by the logical outcome of his own unreasonable utopian madness, his ideas in the Cult of Reason eventually worked their way into the European university system. The de-Christianization utopian ideas birthed in the bloody streets of Paris in the 1790s germinated in Parisian and many European universities. By 1848, these ideas coalesced in Karl Marx's *Communist Manifesto* in which the cult of reason connected to what Marxist philosopher Friedrich Engels called "Scientific Socialism." Here, Christianity and capitalism would be eliminated from the face of the earth through what Engels and Marx called the "dictatorship of the proletariat." This dictatorship would see the oppressed working people of the world unite in socialistic harmony. They would destroy, re-educate, and kill if necessary the "bourgeoisie," eventually ushering in a "stateless" Communist utopian heaven on earth without God, creating a perfect world without war or want.

Many lefty intellectuals in Europe and America were duped by this godless madness supporting the likes of Vladimir Lenin, Joseph Stalin, Mao Zedong, Pol Pot, and Fidel Castro, among many other monsters of Marxism. Fools such as Soviet Premier Nikita Khrushchev still clung to their pie-in-the-sky nonsensical Marxist ideas when he declared in 1961, "I promise Utopia by 1980, where there will be a world without want or war." There are far too many examples of lefty intellectuals falling for the insanity of "Scientific Socialism" to cover in this book, but one classic example is that of the founder of the ACLU, Roger Baldwin, in 1920.

Baldwin was an admirer of the mass murderer socialist Joseph Stalin. After his 1927 visit to the Soviet Union, his 1928 book *Liberty under the Soviets* gives a glowing description of Soviet Socialism. While admitting there were "repressions in Soviet Russia," he believed they were necessary to achieve Stalin's dictatorship of the proletariat in the "transition to socialism" on the road to the long-awaited utopian "Paradise Communism."

I bring up the ACLU founder extensively to show how, 100 years after the founding of the hard-core lefty organization, the ACLU and the Marxist ideas of Roger Baldwin can be found permeated all throughout the lefty intelligentsia, in our universities, and in such organizations as Antifa and BLM in 2020. The ACLU is a BIG supporter of Antifa and BLM. Baldwin's duplicity in typical Orwellian "doublespeak" can be readily seen for what it is when he declared:

> I am for socialism, disarmament, and ultimately for abolishing the state itself as an instrument of violence and compulsion. I seek social ownership of property, the abolition of the propertied class, and sole control by those who produce wealth. Communism is the goal.

As I write about the Marxist mindset of ACLU founder Roger Baldwin, Antifa, BLM, radical lefty Democrats or *mobocrats*, some with full military gear, have taken over the Seattle Police Department's East Precinct and a six-block area in Seattle declaring, "This space is now the property of the people." They claim to be a leaderless entity working for the people to establish racial justice and civil liberties in the state of Washington and eventually America. In reality, this has nothing to do with racial injustice and civil liberties but everything to do with mob-rule and the insanity of cultural Marxism come to fruition in America in 2020. These so-called "peaceful" gun-toting *mobocrats* are the great-great grandchildren of Karl Marx and Roger Baldwin's bizarre dystopian world of lies and their lefty lust for power.

As a so-called pacifist, Baldwin, while using the rhetoric of "liberty," advocated the violence of communism, anarchy, and the "dictatorship of the proletariat." In 1934, as director of the ACLU, Baldwin wrote an article titled "Freedom in the USA and the USSR." In the article, Baldwin exposes the true nature of leftism's worldview:

> But "workers democracy" in action is no product of coercion. It is genuine, and it is the nearest approach to freedom that the workers have ever achieved.

> How long the proletarian dictatorship will last, only world conditions and internal success in building socialism can determine. Highly centralized authority will give way. The State and police power will eventually disappear. Civil liberties will exist again, within the confines of a

socialist society; but not to oppose it, for who will want to? The extension of education, the bringing up of a generation to take active responsibility all over the Soviet Union will lesson power at the center and from the top. The American workers, with no real liberties save to change masters or, rarely, to escape from the working class, could understand their class interests, Soviet "workers' democracy" would be their goal. And if American champions of civil liberties could think in terms of economic freedom as the goal of their labors, they too would accept "workers' democracy" as far superior to what the capitalist world offers to any but a small minority—regretfully, of course— the necessity of the dictatorship while the job of reorganizing society on a socialist basis is being done.

Look at the absolute insanity of Roger Baldwin's naïve unrealistic communist workers worldview. He claims it's not a product of "coercion" while advocating the proletarian dictatorship, and then he says the dictatorship will give way as the state and police will eventually disappear. He then says American workers have no real liberties while Soviet workers have true economic freedom due to "the necessity of dictatorship" so as to reorganize society on a socialist basis.

I know what you're thinking: Roger Baldwin's argument for a "stateless socialist society" is full of contradictions and discombobulated thinking that defy and deny life, liberty, and liberal constitutional democracy. Yes, you are correct— welcome to the bizarre world of leftism, Antifa, socialism, communism, *mobocracy*, and anarchy, as their bunkum-balderdash is an anti-liberty Tower of Babel on the road to slavery.

There is nothing new under the Communist dystopia sun in 2020 as Seattle City Councilwoman Kshama Sawant, a socialist-Trotskyite member of the Socialist Alternative Party, led hundreds of *mobocrats* under the guise of "justice and peace" to take over the Seattle City Hall and subsequently the Seattle Police Department's East Precinct (renaming it the "Seattle Peoples Department") and six city blocks called "Capitol Hill Autonomous Zone," or CHAZ.

Socialist Councilwoman Sawant declared the takeover a "victory" against "the militarized police force of the political establishment and the capitalist state." What Sawant failed to admit was that her political allies who controlled the political establishment were the lefty Democrat mayor of Seattle, Jenny Durkan, and the Democrat chief of police, black American Carmen Best.

This Antifa "CHAZ" was an attempt by these communists, socialists, anarchists, BLM, and *mobocrats* to replicate the Paris Commune of 1871 where French Marxists killed two French army generals defying the French rule of law and controlled Paris for two months. Karl Marx called the "Paris Commune" revolution of 1871 a classic example of his "dictatorship of the proletariat." The problem with these examples of "dictatorships of the proletariat," whether it's 1871 or 2020, they not only don't deal with the real world of human nature without the rule of law, but they also ultimately destroy life and liberty all around it.

Anarchists and communist/socialists are cousins to each other and comrades in arms versus capitalism and liberal democracies. They, like communists, despise free enterprise and believe capitalism is the main source of the exploitation of the working man. They despise all governments except, of course, the "non-temporary government-government" they establish as a means to accomplish its end of the perfect godless, governmentless-stateless society. The anarchy symbol is an "A" with a circle around it with the motto, "No gods, no masters, against all authority."

Anarchists believed communists put too much emphasis on a "temporary" state that will theoretically "wither away," ushering in a communist utopia. Anarchists argue that Marx's dictatorship of the proletariat, the temporary state, creates only a totalitarian state and never truly withers away voluntarily. In theory, they argue for a "leaderless" movement of autonomous individuals creating "autonomous zones" or regions, creating a "non-government government" or a societal structure designed to achieve its utopian goals that will end injustice and establish eternal peace and happiness for all. Did you get that?

The absolutely insane and nonsensical nature of the political philosophies of Antifa, anarchists, and communists is expressed with how they describe their goals. The Oxford Dictionary defines "autonomous" as "a country or region having the freedom to govern itself or control its own affairs." The anarcho-communist Antifa *mobocrats* who have taken over downtown Seattle theoretically believe in a non-coercive society that rejects the state. They believe that autonomous human beings can freely join together in community or "commune" to create the perfect sinless society.

There's only one catch.

It is predicated upon the lie that their society was created with non-violent, non-coercive righteousness and just means to begin with. With violent actions and coercive means, the Antifa-BLM *mobocrats* stole the private property of the Seattle Police Fifth Precinct and took over the control of many businesses within their "non-state of CHAZ," demanding illegal extortion money for their protection. The non-state "CHAZ Staters" had an armed guard "police force" who demanded identification to keep illegal "non-citizens" out and put up a border wall demarcating their "non-State, autonomous State" to be separated from the United States of America with entrance signs declaring, "You are now leaving the USA," "You are now entering Free Cap Hill," and "Capitol Hill Autonomous Zone."

The *mobocrats* marched through their neo-non-state state of CHAZ yelling out, "Show me what democracy looks like!" The *mobocrats* answered back, "This is what democracy looks like!" The stupid Antifa-BLM *mobocrats*, who despise liberal democracy and theoretically dream of a communist utopia, were too foolish to understand that their idiocy was nothing close to what democracy looks like. It is mob-rule and fascism, pure and simple.

Called the "196th Nation" by satirists who saw through their *mobocratic*-infantile insanity, the equally infantile and insane Democratic mayor of Seattle, Jenny Durkan, when asked about the violent nature of the takeover of the

Seattle Police Fifth Precinct and six blocks of her city by Antifa-BLM *mobocrats*, opined that it has a "block party atmosphere" that could turn out to be "a summer of love."

The "summer of love" reference was referring to the summer of 1967 when 100,000 people made their way to San Francisco's Haight-Ashbury to enjoy a carefree summer of drugs, sex, and rock 'n' roll. In 2020, the Antifa-BLM "summer of love" saw thousands of *mobocrats* making their way to Seattle, defying the rule of law and common sense.

Marxists organizations such as Antifa and BLM, working in tandem with radical Democrats, socialists, and anarchists, with weapons in hand, declared they wanted the end of the Seattle Police Department. What did Roger Baldwin desire in his 1934 workers' democracy letter defending the mass murderer Joseph Stalin?

The disappearance of the state and police power.

It is not a coincidence that Marxist organizations such as Antifa and BLM call for defunding of police departments across America. The "Defund the Police" mantra of BLM and many other radical lefty groups is nothing but Orwellian code language for the establishment of a "police state" run by leftists, who will then be able to dictate their political correctness beyond the classroom and culture and into the streets and homes of all Americans. Also, it is not a coincidence that as the radical socialists, Antifa, and BLM *mobocrats* were taking over the heart of Seattle, ACLU lawyers were suing the city of Seattle and the Seattle police for "unnecessary violence."

Such is leftism's perversion of reality and truth.

A few days into the Antifa-BLM communist clown costume play, they realized that their "Seattle commune" or autonomous zone was not so autonomous or independent as they pretended it to be for a few days. At taxpayers' expense, they called for the help of the Seattle Fire Department and Seattle Emergency Services and relied on private free enterprise businesses to provide everything from pizza to Rockstar energy drinks.

Realizing the legal ramifications of designating themselves an "autonomous entity," the *mobocrat* leadership became aware that in their set of demands for free college tuition, free healthcare, and reparations from white citizens, they could not claim "autonomy or independence" from Washington State or the USA as their demands were linked to the money the citizens of those non-CHAZ government entities would provide.

One of the BLM leaders said, "At the end of the day, it can't be an autonomous zone if we're still demanding things from the government, because that would mean we're seceding from their establishment entirely and we have not denounced our American citizenship, and we demand that they pay the fee."

Clever. Use the system while destroying the system with mob-rule.

The Antifa-BLM *mobocrat* leadership also realized, as potential non-citizens of the USA, they would no longer qualify for government social services such as food stamps, welfare, and unemployment. So the clowns of their communist costume party renamed their stolen property or their non-state state "CHOP" or "Capitol Hill Occupied Protest."

"How convenient," said the church lady.

In the early stage of the Seattle *mobocrat* revolution, there was dissension within the ranks as a rich local rapper Solomon Samuel Simone, aka "Raz from CHAZ," declared himself the warlord of CHAZ. With a pistol attached to his hip and an AK-47 slung over his shoulder, he declared in the streets of CHAZ through a megaphone, "This is war!"

One CHAZ comrade protested on social media, "I didn't vote for Raz. I thought we were an autonomous collective? Anarcho-syndicalist commune at the least.... Raz just can't simply expect to wield supreme executive power just because someone threw a sword at him."

Welcome to the lawless world of the "anarcho-syndicalist" commune. Welcome to the world of autonomy where lawlessness defies the democratic rule of law, opening up the floodgates of chaos and *mobocracy*!

Nikkitta Oliver, a radical socialist member of the Seattle Peoples Party, a former mayoral candidate, and a Black Lives Matter activist, assumed a leadership role in the CHOP *mobocracy*. With microphone in hand, she declared the BLM ideological lefty worldview to the crowd of fellow protesting clowns: "We need to align ourselves with the global struggle that acknowledges that the United States plays a role in racialized capitalism ... racialized capitalism is built upon patriarchy, white supremacy, and classism." BLM activist Nikkitta Oliver very succinctly summarized the classic Neo-Marxist worldview.

Documentary filmmaker Ami Horowitz interviewed a large number of Antifa-BLM *mobocrats* in CHAZ, most of whom justified the call for violence and "breaking sh%t" to "destroy F*%^&ing capitalism because white people owned slaves."

Ami Horowitz then asked another self-proclaimed CHAZ leader and BLM activist Jaiden Grayson a number of questions related to the CHAZ Manifesto titled, "Collective Black Voices at Free Capitol Hill to the Government of Seattle, Washington," which was their list of demands from abolishing the police department, the criminal justice system, and the prison system to providing free college education, assigning only black doctors and nurses to take care of black patients, ordering anti-bias training for teachers, and requiring more Marxist black history in the curriculum.

BLM activist Jaiden Grayson told Horowitz, "Every single day I show up here I'm not here to peacefully protest. I'm here to disrupt until my demands are met. You cannot rebuild until you break it all the way down. Respond to the demands of the people or prepare to meet with any means necessary, by any means necessary." When asked if that was just a slogan, Grayson declared, "No! No! No! It's not a slogan; it's not even a warning. I'm letting people know what comes next. A response to violence is not violence itself.... Abolish the police state. The unraveling that happens to that system is also exactly what will fuel the black minds in the black bodies that will recreate a new world."

After telling Horowitz she wanted the criminal justice and prison system abolished, Horowitz concluded the interview by asking, "Do you feel like an American?"

Thinking for a moment, BLM activist Grayson stated, "I am an African brought to America."

While this Ami Horowitz interview with BLM activist Jaiden Grayson might be laughed off as a fringe, juvenile, and sophomoric expression of hardcore left-wing lunacy, or what Horowitz calls a "Confederacy of Dunces," these dunces are no dummies when it comes to disseminating their message and nefarious narrative into the mainstream of American culture and society.

It's why they demand that their anti-Judeo-Christian, Antifa-BLM worldview be taught to our children and the future teachers of our children. If school districts don't comply, they will be attacked by BLM and Antifa as racists, fascists, anti-LGBT, and queer haters. Sadly, school districts across America are kowtowing in the droves to the intimidating politically correct power of hardcore lefty organizations such as Black Lives Matter. They are poisoning the minds of our youth with lies upon lies of bogus history and twisted sociological analysis. More on that latter.

It is not a coincidence that on the "Seattle Police Department East Precinct" sign desecrated in CHOP as "Seattle Peoples Department" hung a sixties-style art print poster of Angela Davis with the title "To the People Power and Equality." Most people don't even remember what kind of radical *mobocrat* Angela Davis was and still is. She spoke in my hometown of Appleton, Wisconsin, on January

20, 2016, on Martin Luther King Jr. Day at Lawrence University. Here is part of what I wrote on that topic in the *RenewAmerica* blog:

> After my non-politically correct speech on Angela Davis at Lawrence University tonight, I went across Lawrence's beautiful campus to hear Dr. Angela Davis' speech. I had 12 in my audience. Angela had 1,200. Why only 12? Maybe because I'm not the Lefty Rock Star Angela is, but it might be because Lawrence University did not want me speaking on campus about the real Angela Davis. I found a Lawrence University Republican student who was able to find me a room at the library, and then with late notice I spoke to an audience of 12.

Besides speaking on the radical revolutionary Communist Angela Davis' worldview and actions, I also spoke of Martin Luther King Jr.'s "I Have a Dream" vision in which Christian culture and character would overcome pigmentation politics and establish the beauty of equality and liberty for ALL as expressed in the Declaration of Independence and defended in the Constitution.

Angela Davis spoke of black lives, Muslim lives, trans lives, lesbian lives, Latino lives, gay lives, and that "ALL lives" mattered, except she did not include Jewish and white lives or those of European heritage. Unfortunately, the mostly white American crowd did not catch that Orwellian perversion of reality. Angela used more identity political labels than the IRS tax code. She spoke on tolerance and diversity, but she showed no tolerance toward Americans of European and Jewish ancestry. She spoke of "black genocide," but not a word on the most horrible genocide in modern history: the Holocaust—the genocide of the children of Israel. We know why. Angela Davis' communist and Black Panther worldview is full of hatred for Jews and whites. This is very typical of the left.

People forget that Angela Davis was a militant member of the Communist Black Panthers and was wanted by the FBI for her possible involvement with the murder of a prison guard in 1970. While acquitted of all charges, Davis continued her advocacy of a Communist revolution in America. Davis not only received an honorary degree from USSR's Moscow State University for her devotion to Marxism, but in 1979 she also received the Lenin Peace Prize (previously called the International Stalin Prize) and was the 1980 and 1984 Communist Party USA candidate for vice president of the United States. Davis' mentor, neo-Marxist Herbert Marcuse of the infamous Marxist Frankfurt School, taught her to never tolerate the "fascist" ideas of the Judeo-Christian worldview, capitalism, and American democracy.

She never did. Comrade Davis spent 40 years in the University of California system teaching her neo-Marxist values to thousands of young Americans who now in turn teach their anti-American values to thousands more across America. Dr. Davis has had a very selective and narrow anti-America understanding of the history of our republic.

Her selective historical narrative is not only racist, but it is also self-serving to the tune of $20,000 per speech. She freely accepts the capital that made her rich in a capitalistic system she has dedicated her life to destroying. Dr. Davis'

Marxist narrative distorts the historical reality of the greatness of our republic. She spoke of Appleton being occupied land by those who were of our Founding Founders heritage. The mostly white liberal crowd loved this Marxist black professor. They adored her, and they absorbed her diatribe against white men and Jews. She praised the 50th anniversary founding of the militant Marxist Black Panthers.

I left disgusted and saddened to know that her neo-Marxist worldview has become predominant in academia and of many of the institutions in the land. The evening's event was endorsed by the Appleton *Post-Crescent*, Lawrence University, Celebrate Diversity Fox Cities, and many churches. How ironic to hear songs about God while their Marxist keynote speaker rejected the God they sang to. How "Twilight Zone-ish" that the audience did not understand the bizarre juxtaposition of Angela Davis' atheistic, Marxist, and racist divisive teachings versus the non-violent teachings of Jesus Christ and Reverend Martin Luther King Jr.

Angela Davis is the godmother of the Black Lives Matter movement, and it is not a coincidence that they have adopted much of her anti-white, anti-Jewish, and anti-American worldview.

Yes, while the CHOP-communist clown show was a comedy of errors worthy of a skit on SNL, it is sadly a tragedy of epic proportions with societal and cultural ramifications that Americans must take action against before this poisonous mob-rule, this communist cancer, continues to spread across the land. This same mob-rule madness happened in Portland, Oregon, as they attacked federal buildings, police departments, businesses, and people as they burned American flags and Bibles in the streets.

These protests and riots have very little to do with race and everything to do with a leftist revolution thrust upon the American people. These "George Floyd riots" are nothing more and nothing less than a Communist-inspired insurrection desiring to not only destroy the presidency of Donald Trump but also literally and ultimately transform the U.S.A.—our republic under God—into the U.S.S.R., the United States of Socialist Republics. To fully understand their nefarious nature and their goal of the U.S.S.R., let's go into more detail about the Marxist origin of Antifa and some of the key players involved in the George Floyd riots in 2020.

Antifa is theoretically on paper an anti-fascist political movement. Supposedly, they are leaderless and autonomous groups, a hodgepodge of amorphous malcontents with the goal of fighting what they deem as fascists and racists in today's society.

Antifa was born in 1932, during the bloody street fights of the German Weimar Republic. The founder, Ernst Thälmann, was a hardcore Stalinist who led the Communist Party of Germany (KPD) and created the Soviet Union–funded "Antifaschistische Aktion" or Antifa. Antifa's primary purpose was to help the KPD fight other political parties to control the streets of the ever-growing political anarchy of Weimar Germany. They fought liberal parties, conservative parties, and anyone who attempted to stop them.

The Marxist Thalmann especially liked to attack the Social Democratic Party of Germany (second largest party in Germany today), which he called "social fascists" because they were too capitalistic. The German communists under Thälmann declared that "fighting fascism means fighting the SPD just as much as it means fighting Hitler and the Christian democracy of Heinrich Brüning's Catholic Centre Party."

Thalmann's Antifa organization was a murdering Marxist organization that was vying for power in Germany. These German Stalinist monsters were also fighting the National Socialist monsters or Nazis. The Antifa-KDP and the Nazis were two evil political parties with two evil political philosophies that despised liberal democracy and the life and liberty that a constitutional republic represented.

Communist Antifa was fighting for ultimate power in Germany. In the end, the German National Socialists or Nazis won out. Many of the members of the German Antifa ended up leaving their losing Communist Party and joined the ranks of the National Socialist Brown Shirts. They were called "Beef Steak Nazis," being brown on the outside and red on the inside. In reality, there really wasn't much difference between the two anti-democratic German socialist parties. Thus, the crossover was easy. Tyranny attracts tyranny.

The anti-fascist mass murderer socialist Joseph Stalin reportedly declared, "Everyone has the right to be stupid, but some people abuse the privilege." Like their namesake, the modern-day Antifa movement, under the guise of fighting "fascism"—i.e., KKK, white supremacy, alt-right, etc.—call all of their ideological opponents "fascists." These "fascists" would include not only the KKK, white supremacists, alt-right, etc., but also Christians, conservatives, traditionalists, Republicans, Libertarians, and anyone who opposes their worldview. They are like their forefather Communist Ernst Thalman, who called all but themselves and their allies "fascists."

In George Orwell's classic dystopian novel *1984*, he describes that "newspeak" occurs "whenever the main purpose of language—which is to describe reality—is replaced by the rival purpose of asserting power over it." That is the purpose of Antifa's so-called "antifascism." It is for power—left-wing authoritarian power to destroy ALL other ideas other than their own lefty utopian nonsense. Antifa-*mobocrats* are the classic totalitarian newspeakers that George Orwell taught us about where the "Ministry of Peace concerns itself with war, the Ministry of Truth with lies, the Ministry of Love with torture, the Ministry of Plenty with starvation, nor do they result from ordinary hypocrisy: they are deliberate exercises in doublethink."

Antifa *mobocrats* use doublethink and newspeak to very cleverly accuse free and democratic individuals and institutions of engaging in "fascism" to further their own fascist authoritarian goals.

Antifa's goal to suppress "fascism" is a child of the neo-Marxist philosopher Herbert Marcuse (remember he was the mentor of Angela Davis). In 1965, Marcuse wrote a very clever tract titled "Repressive Tolerance." In his essay, Marcuse argues that "pure tolerance" favors the political right and "the tyranny of the majority." Therefore, the left—

the "anti-fascists"—are to have "selective tolerance" where they tolerate all ideas in society as long as they concur with their neo-cultural Marxism. According to Marcuse, all the ideas that derive from the Judeo-Christian worldview and traditional conservative values are to be resoundingly rejected, fought against, not tolerated, and labeled as "fascist."

Freedom of speech is fine as long as your speech affirms the cultural-Marxian worldview. Antifa and leftists, in typical Marxist form, pervert the normal use of language in Orwellian and Machiavellian fashion. They distort our Founders' understanding of the First Amendment: legitimate freedom of speech and expression and the right to *peaceably* assemble.

Sadly, we see this intolerant and violent Marxist-fascist mode of operation when many Christians, conservatives, Republicans, and Libertarians attempt to speak on college campuses and are booed down, drummed out, shouted at, or physically attacked, many times not being allowed to finish their speeches.

Lefty historians and politicians very conveniently ignore the Marxist roots of Antifa and attempt to pass them off as legitimate freedom fighters in an attempt to rewrite history, which is blatantly obvious to those who actually know history and aren't duped by lefty lies and deception.

A classic example of passing off Antifa-*mobocrats* as legitimate freedom fighters is lefty Dartmouth historian Mark Bray, a former Occupy Wall Street activist who is an ally and advocate of Antifa *mobocracy*. Bray is the author of the 2017 publication *Antifa: The Anti-Fascist Handbook*.

To sell his Manifesto defending Antifa, Bray appeared on a number of talk shows such as C-Span's *Washington Journal* and NBC's *Meet the Press*. He was also very popular in a large number of magazines and newspapers, even defending Antifa in *Teen Vogue* magazine.

Dr. Bray argues in his book that militant anti-fascism is a legitimate political tradition as he declares in *Antifa: The Anti-Fascist Handbook* that Antifa is "an unabashedly partisan call to arms that aims to equip a new generation of anti-fascists with the history and theory necessary to defeat the resurgent far right."

While many people were appalled by his defense of Antifa's tactics on *Meet the Press*, causing Dartmouth's president to issue a statement distancing the college from any "endorsement of violence," more than 100 members of Dartmouth College signed a letter supporting him. We should not be surprised by that endorsement as the American university is overwhelmingly controlled and indoctrinated by radical lefty academics.

In a *Vox* interview with Sean Illing, Mark Bray, who is passionately sympathetic to Antifa's cause, tells us, "It's also important to remember that these are self-described revolutionaries. They're anarchists and communists who are way outside the traditional conservative-liberal spectrum. They're not interested in and don't feel constrained by conventional norms."

What are the conventional norms that do not constrain Antifa-*mobocrats*? They include tolerance, dialogue, freedom of speech, freedom to peaceably assemble, liberal democracy, and conservative Republican values. Bray goes on to reiterate again to *Vox:* "The other key point, which probably isn't made enough, is that these are revolutionary leftists. They are not concerned about the fact that fascism targets liberalism. These are self-described revolutionaries. They have no allegiance to liberal democracy, which they believed has failed the marginalized communities they're defending."

I want you to clearly understand and hear what Dr. Mark Bray is unabashedly saying and what our republic under God is up against. No true liberal and/or conservative in his or her right mind would defend the illiberal, anti-conservative communist worldview of the Antifa *mobocrats*!

In an interview with *Teen Vogue* magazine—which teaches teens that Marxism is "cool" while America is evil—Antifa apologist Bray downplays their intolerance and violent actions and makes the Antifa-*mobocrats* sound like a combination of Rosa Parks and Martin Luther King Jr. when he says, "Antifa grows out of a larger revolutionary politics that aspires toward creating a better world, but the primary motivation is to stop racists from organizing."

Who is Mark Bray trying to kid? He may fool high schoolers in a teen magazine and college kids who don't know any better, but Antifa's primary goal isn't to "stop racists from organizing." Their *primary goal* is to stop the advancement of the great liberal and conservative ideas that made our republic under God the greatest in world history.

It is also not a coincidence that far too many radical lefty Democrats endorse Antifa and their violent actions, while far too many others remain silent about their violence.

A classic example of that radical affinity of Democrats to Antifa is Democrat Keith Ellison, the first Muslim elected to Congress and the first black American elected to Congress from Minnesota. A convert to Islam at the age of 19, Ellison was an advocate of Louis Farrakhan's anti-Semitic Nation of Islam. He proudly helped organize a Democrat-Minnesota contingent to the racist 1995 Million Man March, which was organized by the white-hating, Jew-hating, Christian-hating racist Louie Farrakhan.

Ellison was not only a defender and advocate Farrakhan's ideas, but he also defended the anti-Semitic remarks of his hero Kwame Ture (Stokely Carmichael), the "honorary prime minister" of the Marxist Black Panthers when he spoke at the University of Minnesota in 1990. Ellison has in the past championed the causes of police murderers Sharif Willis and Mumia Abu-Jamal, and the Marxist murderer hiding from justice in Communist Cuba, Assata Shakur. Ellison advocated for the outright release of Marxist murderer Kathleen Soliah, a Symbionese Liberation Army terrorist who pleaded guilty to the attempted murder of police officers in California.

When Ellison's radical endorsements and activities were exposed during his 2006 run for Congress, he pragmatically distanced himself from the racist Nation of Islam and his radical Marxist comrades—at least in front of the cameras—so he could secure his historic congressional seat.

On January 3, 2018, shortly after Mark Bray's Antifa Manifesto came out, the deputy chairman of the Democratic National Committee Keith Ellison tweeted a picture of himself endorsing Bray's book *Antifa: The Anti-Fascist*

Handbook, tweeting that it "would strike fear into the heart of U.S. President Donald Trump." Ellison had the tweet deleted when he realized he was exposing his radical Marxist-*mobocrat* mindset.

During the George Floyd riots in the streets of St. Paul and Minneapolis in late May and early June 2020, Minnesota's Attorney General Keith Ellison's son, Jeremiah Ellison, a Minneapolis city councilman, proved the old adage that "the acorn doesn't fall far from the tree" when he proudly declared in a tweet, "I hereby declare, officially, my support for ANTIFA." Attorney General Ellison defended his son by saying, "My son's endorsement of Antifa was more of a reaction to the absurd claim that Antifa is a terrorist organization behind the violent destruction of property and death across Minnesota and America." Both Minnesota Democrats denied the violence and killings had anything to do with Antifa-BLM *mobocrats*, saying the "violence and killings" were cause by "white power terrorists."

The Democratic Party of my parents and grandparents has sadly and badly been hijacked by hardcore Jew-hating, white-hating, American-hating leftist *mobocrats* and politicians. Today, far too many Democrat politicians and lefty academics defend Antifa-*mobocrats*, covering up what their true political philosophy really is: FASCISM.

It is not a coincidence that Marxist Ernst Thälmann called all his political opponents "fascists," just as lefties and *mobocrats* do today. Lefties have been calling all their political opponents "fascists" and "Nazis" going back to the 1930s. This is a key part of their political strategy and mode of operation. They did it with Governor Reagan in the

1960s, Nixon, the Bushes, McCain, Romney, Republicans, Conservatives, Christians, Libertarians, and anyone else they deem the enemy. They call us what they are: Fascists.

In reality, it is the left, Antifa, and BLM leadership who think and act in fascist ways while calling their opponents "fascists" and "Nazis." Today's Antifa-BLM *mobocrats* are in our streets in fascist manner, calling for a Marxist revolution as they desire to destroy our republic under God.

I realize that this "Antifa-Black Lives Matter" conflation might be confusing to some readers, but in many cases they not only work together, but they also have similar values, culture, and worldview identification. We've discussed the violent militant origin of Antifa *mobocrats* as a Marxist-Stalinist entity that despises free enterprise and liberal democracy. Now let us turn in more detail to BLM's cultural Marxism.

Chapter 2

Black Lives Matter and Marxism

"We actually do have an ideological frame ... myself and Alicia.... We are trained Marxists."
(Patrisse Cullors)

BLM was created in 2013 and was the brainstorm of three Neo-Marxists: Patrisse Cullors, Alicia Garsa, and Opal Tometi. Cullors, Garcia, and Tometi have all been associated with the Marxist organization the FRSO (Freedom Road Socialist Organization), one of the largest radical left groups in America along with the Democratic Socialists of America, Committees of Correspondence for Democracy and Socialism, and the Communist Party USA. The FRSO is a Marxist-Leninist group coming out of the Maoist tradition and is the guiding force behind BLM. Changing its name to Liberation Road, their website declares,

> Among the things we draw from Marx: the analysis of how capitalism works and why it is a dynamic but irrational system; and of class struggle as the

motor force of history. Marx and Engels believed
that working people are capable of overturning
capitalism and creating a society based on human
need not profit. They learned from the rise and
smashing of the Paris Commune that workers
could create incredible democratic governance
forms but must be prepared to defend them with
weapons against exploiters grabbing back power.

Notice the call for overturning capitalism, learning from
the "Paris Commune" in being prepared to defend workers
with weapons against grabbing back power. It is why BLM
and Antifa are "comrades-in-arms"—they have many of the
same common goals.

They go on to say in their website:

From Lenin: an understanding of imperialism—
of the revolutionary potential unleashed when
oppressed nations struggle for self-determination,
and of the tendency of socialists in imperialist
countries to fall into reformism and support
their own bourgeoisies in imperialist wars. Lenin
also emphasized that the capitalist state must be
completely destroyed and he made breakthroughs
in building a revolutionary party—for which there
is definitely no everlasting formula!

Notice the Leninist call: "That the capitalist state must be
completely destroyed."

So while BLM has a rhetorical façade of fighting for
democracy and justice, it is a front group for a number of

hardcore leftist/Marxist organizations that call for the destruction of our republic under God.

BLM co-founder Alicia Garza was born in 1981 and describes herself as a "queer social justice activist." One of her heroes is Assata Shakur. Shakur is a Communist revolutionary, a former Black Panther, and a member of the Black Liberation Army. In 1972, Shakur killed a New Jersey state trooper and was convicted of murder in 1977. In 1979, Shakur escaped prison and fled to Communist Cuba where she still lives to this day. Shakur is a BLM hero and a role model for BLM co-founder Alicia Garza, who proudly says of her murdering Marxist idol, "When I use Assata's powerful demand in my organizing work, I always begin by sharing where it comes from, sharing about Assata's significance to the Black Liberation Movement, what its political purpose and message is, and why it's important in our context."

In context, Alica Garza's hero and mentor is a proud Marxist police murderer, still on the FBI's most wanted terrorist list, who is hiding from justice in Communist Cuba. No wonder during the summer of 2020 BLM activists had no problem destroying millions of dollars of property and hurting, beating, and/or killing a number of innocent people.

Before I go on to illustrate the call for violence and violent activity of BLM leadership, it is important to remember that the majority of the black American community repudiate BLM's violent rhetoric and actions.

Barbara Ann Reynolds, a black journalist, an author of a notable biography of Jesse Jackson, and a 1960s civil rights activist, wrote an August 24, 2015, article for the *Washington Post* in which she reflects this baby boomer's serious concerns of the militant nature of the Marxist leadership in BLM. Reynolds writes:

> The baby boomers who drove the success of the civil rights movement want to get behind Black Lives Matter, but the group's confrontational and divisive tactics make it difficult. In the 1960s, activists confronted white mobs and police with dignity and decorum, sometimes dressing in church clothes and kneeling in prayer during protests to make a clear distinction between who was evil and who was good.

> But at protests today, it is difficult to distinguish legitimate activists from the mob actors who burn and loot. The demonstrations are peppered with hate speech, profanity, and guys with sagging pants that show their underwear. Even if the BLM activists aren't the ones participating in the boorish language and dress, neither are they condemning it.

Ms. Reynolds is 100 percent spot on when she says, "It is difficult to distinguish legitimate activists from mob actors who burn and loot." Ms. Reynolds understands that *mobocrats* with no dignity and decorum have peppered the demonstrations with hate speech, and that sadly many BLM leaders aren't condemning it. This is not what Martin Luther King's SCLC (Southern Christian Leadership Conference) taught, nor was it what James Farmer's CORE (Congress of Racial Equality) exemplified during the 1961 Freedom Rides.

BLM co-founder Patrisse Cullors was born in Los Angeles, California, in 1984. Like her Marxist BLM colleague Alicia Garza, Cullors also considers herself a "queer social justice activist" and a "trained Marxist." Quoting the BLM website, they are dedicated to "engage comrades" in "affirming a queer-affirming network" so as to "disrupt the Western-prescribed nuclear family structure" and "dismantle cisgender privilege and uplift black trans folk."

To "disrupt the Western-prescribed nuclear family" reminds me of January 15, 1987, when Jesse Jackson, along with 500 lefty *mobocrat* demonstrators at Stanford University, declared, "Hey, hey, ho, ho, Western Civ has to go!" Jackson's mob demanded that the university would no longer teach "white-centric" Western civilization and would replace it with the lefty dogma of multiculturalism, identity politics, and black studies. It is not a coincidence that the neologism *cisgender* or *cissexual* originates from German Marxist sexologist Volkmar Sigusch, who was a student of neo-Marxists Theodor Adorno and Max Horkheimer of the infamous Frankfurt School of Marxist Social Research.

Patrisse Cullors also has the distinction of being trained as a militant activist by Eric Mann of the domestic terrorist group the Marxist Weather Underground of Bill Ayers and Bernadine Dohrn infamy, the "non-friend friends" of Barack Obama.

In 2015, during an interview on the Real News Network with fellow Marxist professor Dr. Jared Ball (who pushes *Black Marxism* by Cedric J. Robinson on his website, among other Marxist works), Patrisse Cullors spoke of her and BLM co-founder Alicia Garza's "super versed" ideological training in Marxism.

When I posted this "Marxist revelation" on social media, a black friend, a one-time colleague of mine and a BLM advocate, appeared quite upset and agitated by my claims of BLM "ideological training in Marxism."

He asked me this question: "So are you calling Black Lives Matter a Marxist organization?"

He went on to post the following retort to my claim:

> I guess the power of the Black Lives Matter protest around the world is upsetting the proverbial apple cart. This morning, I read on a person's page [Jake Jacobs] that he believes that BLM is a MARXIST organization [caps his]. His proof, a video that he got off the internet. Afterward, I asked if he really believed this, another person who I have known for years, chirps in and calls BLM a domestic terrorist organization. I wonder if they would consider the Continental Congress a domestic terrorist organization?

> Both of these people love to quote Dr. Martin Luther King and how he would be ashamed at the BLM movement. The funny thing is this: white America was saying the exact same thing about the Southern Christian Leadership Conference in 1967 and 1968. Since people like this love Dr. King, I will leave you with my favorite quote by him: "The two most dangerous things in the world today are sincere ignorance and conscious stupidity." I

ponder on which side of the moral spectrum they
stand. Dr. King, thank you for your wisdom and
discernment.

I could tell my friend what quite upset me with my "Marxist"
description of BLM leadership, which he considered immoral
and full of either "sincere ignorance or conscious stupidity."
Here is how I responded to his question:

> I'm glad to see you ask me that question and to
> see your post in relation to it. Why do I ask? It
> means you, like myself, have a serious problem
> with Marxism (I was hoping that was the case)
> as it is a vile and violent "ideological frame and
> theory" that is anti-Christian, anti-life and liberty.
> That is a good thing to see. Your question was
> "So are you calling Black Lives Matter a Marxist
> organization?" You should note that I differentiated
> the BLM Leadership from the peaceful protesters
> when I said "Most of the peaceful protesters
> have good hearts with good intentions that want
> equality & justice for all in America but are being
> duped & used by BLM Marxists leaders." When
> you study the co-founders of BLM you will find
> they have many connections to various Marxist
> organizations. Have you ever heard of Dr. Jared
> Ball? As I write this he just put this tweet above a
> painting of George Floyd on Twitter declaring the
> "Principles of slavery still at core of U.S.' socio-
> economic order." Dr. Ball's website pushes books
> on Marxism and has podcasts such as "Millennials
> Are Killing Capitalism." Dr. Ball is a Marxist
> Professor of Communications at Morgan State

University and he interviewed the co-founder of BLM Patrisse Cullors in 2015. In the interview he asks her this question. (It is long to give you FULL context)

BALL: Some people, including—you know we have, a number of people have reached out, including political prisoner Jalil Muntaqim, who has written from behind the prison walls trying to reach out to Black Lives Matter activists and others. And one of the critiques that he shared—a loving critique, as I would want to point out, by the way—is that he was concerned or is concerned that there's a lack of perhaps ideological direction in Black Lives Matter that would allow it to be, to fizzle out in, as he said, in comparison to Occupy Wall Street. As you advance in your own organization, as you all are headed to Cleveland to participate in this Black Lives Movement conference, how do you respond to that particular critique? Again, a loving critique from an elder of the struggle that some others share, that I've even shared as well, to be frank, as a concern in part because of the co-optation and the appropriation, that a more clear ideological structuring might be of some value here. But how do you respond to those kinds of again, loving criticisms?'

Here is her VERY revealing Marxist answer:

CULLORS: Um, I think that the criticism is helpful.... I think of a lot of things. The first thing, I think, is that we actually do have an ideological

42

frame. Myself and Alicia in particular are trained organizers. We are trained Marxists. We are super-versed on, sort of, ideological theories. And I think that what we really tried to do is build a movement that could be utilized by many, many black folk. We don't necessarily want to be the vanguard of this movement. I think we've tried to put out a political frame that's about centering who we think are the most vulnerable amongst the black community, to really fight for all of our lives. And I do think that we have some clear direction around where we want to take this movement.

Notice something VERY important to this interview:

Dr. Ball, a Marxist advocate, brings up fellow Marxist "prisoner Jalil Muntaqim."

Dr. Ball is saying that there is loving concern by other Marxists like Jalil Muntaqim—a Black Panther/Black Liberation Army Marxist in prison for murdering two NYPD officers—that you don't have an "ideological direction" or an "ideological structure."

Notice how the co-founder/leader of BLM answers:

The first thing, I think, is that we actually do have an ideological frame. Myself and Alicia in particular are trained organizers. We are trained Marxists. We are super-versed on, sort of, ideological theories.

Cullors defends the BLM worldview by saying they actually do have an ideological structure that she/Alicia Garza are super versed in: MARXISM. This source is a left-wing BLM advocate and a Marxist advocate himself. Even the black national spokesperson of CORE (Congress of Racial Equality) Niger Innis says, like I do, that BLM leadership works from a "Marxist ideological frame/structure/direction."

Sadly, the majority of the BLM well-meaning peaceful protesters don't realize that.

I hope this Marxist truth about BLM doesn't upset you. I believe your heart is for truth and justice. I will pray for your strength in dealing with this revelation. We must all join together to make sure that the militant Marxist leadership of BLM doesn't harm millions of good people who peaceably assemble for Christianity and liberal democracy versus Marxism and violence. Shalom, my brother in Christ and liberty!

I can only hope and pray that someday my friend and many more like him with good hearts and good intentions will see the antithetical and counterproductive nature of Marxism in achieving authentic civil rights as preached and practiced by Martin Luther King Jr., James Farmer, Whitney Young, and the great black liberal anti-communist Roy Wilkins. Wilkins exposed Marxist leaders within the civil rights movement such as Communist Dictator Joseph Stalin's friend and admirer Paul Robeson, the famous black American singer.

Comrade Cullors ("Comrade" is a BLM term used on their website) is more than just trained in Marxist ideology; she is also an unabashed supporter of the Palestinian terrorist organization Hamas and is a signer of the "2015 Black

Solidarity Statement with Palestine," which calls for a boycott of Israeli goods and anti-Israel political pressure, declaring, "From the river to the sea, Palestine must be free." In other words, it calls for the elimination of the State of Israel. It is interesting to note that BLM activists love to use the word *genocide* for Israel and the Jews while they endorse the anti-Semitism of Hamas and other Palestinian terrorists.

During the BLM George Floyd riots on May 30, 2020, in Los Angeles, California, Cullors led the BLM activists and targeted upper-class and Jewish neighborhoods in Beverly Hills and the Fairfax District near a popular high-end retail mall called the Grove to attack the "heart of capitalism." Paintings of George Floyd wearing a Palestinian keffiyeh and signs saying, "F...K Israel" were carried by the BLM *mobocrats*.

A BLM colleague, Melina Abdullah, a professor of Pan-African Studies at Cal State LA and BLM-LA co-founder, grabbed the bullhorn from Cullors declaring, "F**k white capitalism! F**K the police! F**k the Grove!"

Cullors and Abdullah were elated to see violent demonstrations in the streets of Los Angeles, California, especially the Fairfax District and Beverly Hills area, as she tweeted, "This is an uprising. A rebellion. A revolt." As police were being attacked and hurt, so were many innocent bystanders while businesses were being ransacked and burnt to the ground. Professor Abdullah proudly declared,

> We've been very deliberate in saying that the
> violence and pain and hurt that's experienced
> on a daily basis by black folks at the hands of a

repressive system should also be visited upon, to a degree, to those who think that they can just retreat to white affluence.

It is not a coincidence that Abdullah's colleague Dr. Anthony Ratcliff, an Antifa and BLM activist, started a campaign demanding that Dr. Abdullah become the dean of ethnic studies and that BLM curriculum be mandated at Cal State LA to fight "anti-blackness and white supremacy" on campus.

A BLM strategy is to bring their Marxist revolution to more schools and to white suburbs and business districts to awaken them to their "oppression" upon black America. Dr. Abdullah has a hateful résumé of supporting and appearing at Hitler-loving, Jew-hating Louis Farrakhan's Nation of Islam events and is an unabashed attacker of Israel and the Jewish people. She had no problem when the heavily Jewish area of Fairfax District was violently attacked by BLM rioters. They sprayed graffiti on the walls of the Temple Beth Israel synagogue that read, "Free Palestine" and "f*** Israel." A statue of Raoul Wallenberg, the Swedish diplomat who saved thousands of Hungarian Jews from the Nazis, was also smeared with anti-Semitic slogans by the BLM *mobocrats.*

During the George Floyd riots, BLM *mobocrats* declared that white America was involved in "genocide" against black America as they desecrated statues of President Washington and other presidents, spray painting "genocide" on them.

Genocide?! Are they nuts?! What planet are they from?

Not only does the anti-Semitic BLM organization hypocritically act out against Jews and Israel, but they also insult them for the memory of a true genocide—the Holocaust—when six million Jews were exterminated by the Nazis. BLM clearly does not understand the definition of the word *genocide* as they cheapen its meaning by falsely applying it to America in 1619, 1776, and today.

On July 19, 2015, a group of BLM *mobocrats*, who were trained in Marxist Saul Alinsky tactics, shut down the speeches of two Democratic candidates for president, Bernie Sanders and Martin O'Malley, at a Phoenix, Arizona, NetRoots Nation convention of progressives. The leader of this *mobocratic* disruption who would not let the Democratic candidates speak while screaming out, "Burn everything down! Shut this s**t down! Rise the f**k up!" was none other than the Marxist BLM co-founder Patrisse Cullor.

In July 2016, Cullors called for, if necessary, the use of violence to shut down the Republican Presidential Convention. In an August 2017 interview with the *Los Angeles Times*, Cullors said that BLM would never talk to President Trump because he was like Adolf Hitler:

> We wouldn't as a movement take a seat at the table with Trump because we wouldn't have done that with Hitler. Trump is literally the epitome of evil, all the evils of this country—be it racism, capitalism, sexism, homophobia.... And if I'm thinking about what I want my children to know in 30, 40, 50 years, I want them to know that I resisted a president at all costs, because this

president literally tried to kill our communities,
and is killing our communities.

Besides the intellectually weak and *ad hominem–reductio
ad Hitlerum* argument, notice communist Cullors' disdain
for "capitalism."

BLM co-founder Opal Tometi was born in Phoenix, Arizona,
in 1984. Tometi was the former executive director of Black
Alliance for Just Immigration (BAJI), a George Soros–
funded organization. It is a documented front group for
the Freedom Road Socialist Organization (FRSO), which
has the ultimate goal of destroying America's liberal
democracy by creating a socialist United States of America.
FRSO members are advocates of Harry Haywood's "Black
Belt Republic," the call for an autonomous black nation
in the American Deep South in the 1920s and 30s. Harry
Haywood was a black American and a leading figure in the
Communist Party USA (CPUSA) and the Communist Party
of the Soviet Union (CPSU). He supported Communist
Dictator Joseph Stalin's goal of destroying liberal
democracy and establishing a one-world communist utopia.
Haywood's 1978 autobiography *Black Bolshevik* is admired
by today's Marxist BLM advocates as it connects "African
American oppression to the Marxist-Maoists solution to
liberate Blacks from White control."

In December 2015, Black Lives Matter sent a delegation
with co-founder Opal Tometi to act as "observers" during
the Venezuelan Parliamentary elections. The Venezuelan
Marxist Maduro did not allow for observers from the
OAS, EU, or UN. The only accepted "observers" were

from regimes and organizations friendly to the Marxist "revolutionary cause."

BLM leader Tometi praised Maduro and his socialist system. Tometi attacked Bernie Sanders for daring to call Hugo Chavez a "dead communist dictator," and she attacked Hillary Clinton for not supporting the socialist leader Maduro. Opal Tometi admires Chavez and Maduro and loves the phrase stamped on Venezuelan made products, "*HECHO EN SOCIALISMO*," or "Made in SOCIALISM." On December 26, 2015, Tometi wrote a letter to the *Black Agenda Report* in which she praises Venezuela while condemning the United States. Tometi wrote,

> In these last 17 years, we have witnessed the Bolivarian Revolution champion participatory democracy and construct a fair, transparent election system recognized as among the best in the world—a democratic process that has advocated the rights of Afro Descendants and other oppressed people within Venezuela and across the globe.

Anybody who knows anything about Venezuelan politics knows that BLM co-founder Opal Tometi was lying about Venezuelan Marxist Dictator Nicolas Maduro and his so-called democratic process.

Protestors at BLM events are notorious for vile, vitriolic, and incendiary rhetoric directed at policemen, cisgender white males, and heterosexual Christians and conservatives who are attacked as Nazis and fascists. At a December 2014 march, BLM *mobocrats* chanted in unison: "What do we want? Dead cops. When do we want it? Now!" At an August

2015 rally, BLM *mobocrats* cried out: "Pigs in a blanket, fry'em like bacon!" You don't have to wonder where Colin Kaepernick got his idea to wear socks depicting the police as pigs. In November 2015, about 150 BLM *mobocrats* in fascistic style stormed the Dartmouth University's library screaming, "Black Lives Matter! F**k you, you filthy white f**ks! F**k you and your comfort! F**K you, you racist sh**!"

In late 2016, the co-founder of Toronto Canada's BLM's branch, Yusra Khogali, posted a horrible diatribe against white people on Facebook:

> Whiteness is not humxness. in fact, white skin is sub-humxn.... White ppl are recessive genetic defects. this is factual. white ppl need white supremacy as a mechanism to protect their survival as a people because all they can do is produce themselves. black ppl simply through their dominant genes can literally wipe out the white race if we had the power to.

In February of 2016, Khogali posted a violent threat to a Toronto police officer on Facebook: "The police officer who killed Andrew Loku. We. Are coming for you. U better believe it. You are going to spend the rest of your life without your family like how Andrew Loku's 5 children will have to go on without their father. Justice will be served."

Around that same time, she tweeted: "Plz Allah give me strength to not cuss/kill these men and white folks out here today. Plz plz plz." In February of 2017, at the Toronto U.S. Consulate, Khogali attacked Liberal Prime Minister Justin Trudeau as a "white supremacist terrorist."

While this violent racist rhetoric by BLM leadership and activists does not indict the majority of BLM participants with good intentions, it does express and reflect a very destructive worldview. If led to its logical conclusion, we will not see the fulfillment of Martin Luther King Jr.'s dream but its demise and the death of liberal democracy in America.

Hawk Newsome, chairman of BLM's Greater New York chapter, in an interview with the *Daily Mail*, revealed that they are training "military special forces" to lead the "war on police." Newsome said, "We pattern ourselves after the Black Panthers, after the Nation of Islam, we believe we need to arm ourselves." It is not a coincidence that Newsome invoked the militant Marxist Black Panthers or the anti-Semitic, white-hating Nation of Islam.

During an interview on Fox News' *The Story*, Martha MacCallum asked Newsome, "You ... have said that violence is sometimes necessary in these situations.... What exactly is it that you hope to achieve through violence?"

Newsome responded,

> I said if this country doesn't give us what we want, then we will burn down this system and replace it. All right? And I could be speaking ... figuratively. I could be speaking literally. It's a matter of interpretation. Let's observe the history of the 1960s, when black people were rioting we had the highest growth in wealth, in property ownership. Think about the last few weeks since we started protesting. There have been eight cops fired across the country.... I don't condone nor do I condemn rioting but I'm just telling you what I observed.

Toward the end of the interview, MacCallum read a quote from Martin Luther King Jr. when he was speaking to the Southern Christian Leadership Conference in 1967. MacCallum asked Newsome if he agreed with King's quote: "Let us be dissatisfied until that day when nobody will shout, 'White power!' when nobody will shout, 'Black power!' but everybody will talk about God's power and human power."

Newsome responded, "I love the Lord and my Lord and Savior Jesus Christ is the most famous black radical revolutionary in history. And he was treated just like Dr. King. He was arrested on occasion and he was also crucified or assassinated. This is what happens to black activists. We are killed by the government." At the end of the interview, Newsome told MacCallum, "I just want black liberation and black sovereignty, by any means necessary."

When dissected, this interview with BLM leader Hawk Newsome is classic Orwellian doublespeak, with the manipulation of language and verbal sleight of hand. He tells us in other interviews that BLM patterns itself not on the non-violent teachings of Martin Luther King Jr. and the teaching of Jesus Christ, but on the militant Marxist Black Panthers and the racist Nation of Islam labeled by the leftist organization Southern Poverty Law Center as an anti-Jewish, anti-LGBT hate group.

This is a very strange contradiction for a BLM leader who says he "loves his Lord and Savior Jesus Christ," a Jewish rabbi who taught non-violence and was not a "black radical revolutionary." Newsome then goes on to justify 1960s black rioting as "creating a growth in wealth and property ownership." Nothing could be further from the truth; it was not rioting that created prosperity for black Americans in the 1960s—it was disciplined hard work, coupled with federal laws such as the 1964 Civil Rights Act, the 1965 Voting Rights Act, and the 1968 Housing Act, that broke the institutional racism of Democratic Jim Crow laws that had been entrenched in America since the 1870s.

In Newsome's doublespeak, he says he is for peace, and yet he says, "I don't condone nor do I condemn rioting." Then, in classic postmodern sleight of hand gobbledygook, he says, "If this country doesn't give us what we want, then we will burn down this system and replace it. All right? And I could be speaking ... figuratively. I could be speaking literally. It's a matter of interpretation." A matter of interpretation?! Literally, "literally" means "literal, actual, going to do." What does he say BLM is going to do? "Burn down the system and replace it" with "black liberation, black sovereignty, by any means necessary."

Newsome's language is classic black Marxist rhetoric. The brilliance of our Founders in 1776 was not to call for the "sovereignty" of a race of people, but to declare that "ALL men are created equal." Sovereignty of the people was meant to be the great equalizer for all, not the call for a separate "race" or "class" of people to control another. It is human sovereignty under God's sovereignty that matters, not "white sovereignty," "black sovereignty," or any sovereignty outside of the realm of advancing all of humanity, not just a select race.

The phrase used by Newsome, "by any means necessary," was used in a speech by one of BLM's intellectual heroes, the Marxist Franz Fanon in 1960, at a Positive Action Conference in Accra, Ghana. In his speech titled "Why We Use Violence," Fanon concluded that to achieve the desired goal of black freedom from white (British) rule, "ending the colonial regime by any means necessary" might demand violence.

This Fanon phrase was popularized by Malcolm X in a 1965 speech in which he said, "We declare our right on this earth to be a man, to be a human being, to be respected as a human being, to be given the rights of a human being in this society, on this earth, in this day, which we intend to bring into existence *by any means necessary*." A picture of Malcolm X carrying an M1 carbine in his right hand and pulling back the blinds in his Queens, New York, home to keep watch from possible assassins was in *Life* and *Ebony* magazines in 1964. By 1966, it became a popular poster with the title, "BY ANY MEANS NECESSARY." It soon became a slogan used by the Black Panthers and many other black liberation advocates. The slogan is also often used for BLM leadership and advocates.

The use of this phrase "by any means necessary" feeds the violent tendencies protestors have in the heat of the moment that turn into a mob. Here, *mobocratic* passions kill and injure many innocent police and destroy the businesses and properties of those in the mob's path. History is replete with peaceful assemblies turning into a mob due to passions or a mixture of peaceful protesters mixing with *mobocrats* who are hell bent on death and destruction. Such is the mode of operation of Antifa and far too many BLM activists who thrive on violence.

This is why Martin Luther King, Rosa Parks, and most civil rights advocates of the 1960s hated the phrase "by any means necessary," for they understood its potential to be profoundly counterproductive, creating violence and anti-democratic activities. Martin Luther King often said, "We must forever conduct our struggle on the high plane of dignity and discipline. We must not allow our creative protest to degenerate into physical violence."

Unfortunately, BLM violence has become commonplace in America.

One of the most dangerous comments from BLM's Newsome was that "Jesus Christ is the most famous black radical revolutionary in history." It is reminiscent of Barack Obama's pastor Jeremiah Wright, when he declared in 2008, "Jesus was a poor black man who lived in a country and who lived in a culture that was controlled by rich white people. The Romans were rich. The Romans were Italians, which means they were Europeans, which means they were white. And the Romans ran everything in Jesus' country."

On October 10, 2015, at the twentieth anniversary of the anti-Semitic Nation of Islam's Million Man March "Justice or Else" rally, Barack Obama's former pastor Jeremiah Wright declared:

> The same issue is being fought today and has been fought since 1948 [the rebirth of the State of Israel], and historians are carried back to the 19th century ... when the original people, the Palestinians—and please remember, Jesus was a Palestinian—the Palestinian people had the Europeans come and take their country.

To remove Judaism from the Rabbi Jesus and make him black or a Palestinian is a common practice by BLM activists.

On June 22, 2020, during the BLM-Antifa protests and riots, BLM activist Shaun King tweeted, "Yes, I think the statues of the white European they claim is Jesus should also come down. They are a form of white supremacy. Always have been, In the Bible, when the family of Jesus wanted to hide, and blend in, guess where they went? EGYPT! Not Demark. Tear them down." King's ideas about Jesus are expressing BLM's anti-Christian worldview.

King went on to say that "white Jesus is a lie" and a "tool of white supremacy" created to help white people use Christianity as a "tool of oppression." King added that "white people would never have accepted a religion from a brown man" and that "all murals and stained glass windows of white Jesus, and his European mother, and their white friends should also come down. They are a gross form of white supremacy. Created as tools of oppression. Racist propaganda. They should all come down." So essentially, he means tear down "white churches."

Let's deal first with BLM activist Shaun King's claim that "white Jesus is a lie." It's interesting to note that like Barack Obama, Shaun King's mother is white and he has been accused of lying about having a black father. But back to the "white Jesus is a lie."

My thesis for my M.A. in Judeo-Christian historical studies at Ashland Theological Seminary was titled, "The Historical and Theological Jewish Context of Jesus' Day." It is true that Jesus was not "white" or of European ancestry. Jesus, or his

Hebrew name *YeShua*, was born as a Jew circa 3 B.C. in the land of Israel (not Palestine, as that area would not be called "Palestine" or "Syria-Palestina" until 135 A.D. by the Jew-hating Emperor Hadrian). He was born in the Jewish town of Bethlehem, Judea. The Hebrew for Judea derives from the Hebrew word *Yehudah* or Jew. Thus, Judea means "land of the Jews." Jews had an inextricable soul connection to the land of Israel in relationship to the covenant with their God, YAHWEH. They even called themselves "Israel."

The Bible tells us that Jesus, being Jewish, was circumcised on the eighth day in accordance with Jewish custom and was an orthodox practitioner of the *Torah*—Jewish law. Jesus' parents, Mary (or *Miriam* in Hebrew) and Joseph (or *Yoseph* in Hebrew), were Jewish through and through. Jesus spoke Hebrew, the language of the Jews. Jesus or *YeShua* was a rabbi or a teacher of the Torah, the Jewish scriptures from Genesis to Malachi. On the Jerusalem cross of His redemption for mankind was a *"Titulus Crucis"* or title on the cross, which said in Hebrew, Greek, and Latin, *"Iēsus Nazarēnus, Rēx Iūdaeōrum—Jesus the Nazarene, King of the Jews."*

So, Shaun King, Jesus was not "white" or European, but neither was he "black" or African. He was Jewish. Your call to destroy all "white" representations in statues, paintings, and stained glass windows of Jesus across America is not only a call to violate the law with the destruction of public and private property, but it is also a call to destroy what those artifacts symbolically represent: *the Judeo-Christian worldview.* When you declare that white people would not accept "a religion from a brown man," you are categorically and undeniably wrong.

Throughout the ages, millions of white people have accepted the religion of the Jew Jesus who probably had olive-colored skin, being a Galilean Jew from Israel. When Jesus Christ truly lives in the hearts and minds of believers, they know that they are called not to oppress but to love their neighbors. It is not a coincidence that the overwhelming number of abolitionists and civil rights activists who were white, brown, black, and every color in between were Christians, followers of the loving teachings of the Jew, Jesus Christ. Many cultures throughout the ages have depicted Jesus in ways that resembled their tribe, their community, and their culture. Ethiopia has depicted Jesus as black for more than 1,500 years. Images of Jesus appearing Asian are throughout Asian history and culture. Many African Americans churches show Jesus as black. What's ultimately behind BLM activist Shaun King's call to destroy "white Jesus" is the neo-Marxist call to destroy the Judeo-Christian foundation of our nation.

When black pastors such as Jeremiah Wright call Jesus a "Palestinian" and join in with the anti-Semitic, anti-Israel Nation of Islam's Louis Farrakhan's diatribes against the people of Israel, we are exposed to the ugly Jew hate that festers in the teachings of many black liberation pastors and activists who declare, "From the river to the sea, Palestine must be free"—in other words, no more land of Israel.

When we are told by BLM leaders and activists that Jesus was a "black radical revolutionary," we are hearing the ideological worldview of the Marxist Black Liberation Movement and Marxist Black Liberation Theology.

We covered some Marxist aspects of the Black Liberation Movement with Marxists Assata Shakurr and Jalil Muntaqim, but what is Black Liberation Theology? Black Liberation Theology was born from the womb of Marxist Liberation Theology, which views Jesus through the lens and ideological framework of Marxism. Liberation Theology was primarily a Roman Catholic Latin American phenomenon from the 1950s and 1960s. It was an amalgamation of Christian theology and a Marxist social-economic analysis with a call for "revolutionary action" with more of an emphasis on Karl Marx than Jesus Christ.

A classic example of the clash between an anti-Marxist Catholic and passionate pro-Marxist Liberation Theology Catholic was on March 4, 1983, at the welcoming ceremonies for Pope John Paul II at the airport in Managua, Nicaragua. With Marxist-Leninist President Daniel Ortega standing next to him, Pope John Paul II was greeted by Nicaraguan Catholic priest Ernesto Cardenal. When he tried to kiss the ring of the Pontiff, John Paul II wagged his finger in Cardenal's face and ordered him to quit his post as the "Marxist minister of culture and revolutionary government."

Pope John Paul II had a particular disdain for Marxism. He understood the evil nature of Marxism that he had experienced in his native land of Poland through the evil reign of Joseph Stalin and the Soviet Union. In response to the admonishment by the Pope, Cardenal declared, "Christ led me to Marx. I do not think the Pope understands Marxism.... For me the four Gospels are equally Communist. I am a Marxist who believes in God, follows Christ and is a revolutionary for the sake of the Kingdom."

Pope John Paul II, with a doctorate in sacred theology
and philosophical studies, understood perfectly well the
destructive ideological framework of Marxism and its
anti-Christian worldview. Never mind the contradiction
when Karl Marx and Fredrich Engels declared that their
"scientific socialism" was by its very nature atheistic and
anti-Christian. Pope John Paul II understood that to mix
Marx with Christ was like mixing ammonia and bleach,
creating a "toxic gas" in church polity that would poison
humanity.

The theoretical ideological synthesis between Christ and
Marx was made popular in America by the "father" of Black
Liberation Theology, Dr. James H. Cone. Dr. Cone's works
had a profound influence not only on Reverend Jeremiah
Wright and President Barack Obama, but also on many
"black liberation" groups. Cone's books from 1969, *Black
Theology and Black Power*; 1970, *A Black Theology of
Liberation*; and 1980, *The Black Church and Marxism*, are
but a few of his works that articulate his mixing of Marx
and Jesus.

In his book *Black Theology and Black Power*, Cone
declared, in a very unchristian manner, "The time has come
for white America to be silent and listen to black people
... all white men are responsible for white oppression....
Theologically, Malcolm X [a Muslim] is not far from wrong
when he called the white man the 'devil.'" In June 1984,
James Cone and Barack Obama's Pastor Jeremiah Wright,
among many other black American church leaders, attended
a conference in Communist Cuba where they praised
Communist Dictator Fidel Castro and exchanged ideas on
the need for Marxism in American culture.

Reverend Cone preached that white churches in America were based on "white supremacy" and not the gospel of Jesus Christ. Therefore, "the gospel of Jesus Christ" needed Karl Marx's "ideological framework" to explain the system of the white oppressor class versus the victim class, black Americans. James Cone denied key Christian doctrines such as substitutionary atonement and redemption for sin. To the Marxist Cone, Jesus was not the savior and redeemer of all of the world, as understood in classic Christian orthodoxy, but a radical revolutionary sent to give oppressed blacks social justice empowerment over whites.

In *Black Theology: An International Journal*, Liam Miller's February 2020 article "James Cone's Constructive Vision of Sin and the Black Lives Matter Movement" states,

> The Black Lives Matter movement faces persistent opposition by those who shift the discussion from structural and societal inequality toward individual responsibility. This socio-political outworking of a universalised and individualised doctrine of sin is common amongst White, conservative Christian communities. James H. Cone's constructive doctrine of sin is an alternative in the contemporary context. For Cone, sin is particularly expressed based on the concrete existence of a community, and its overcoming is bound up in the oppressed struggle for liberation and the affirmation of their humanity. This paper explores Cone's community conception of sin, demonstrating its power to combat the idol of Whiteness and equip churches to take practical

steps to ensure that Black lives matter in a White society.

Thus, it's not a coincidence that the BLM leadership today readily adapts and articulates Cone's theological Marxist concept of "the idol of Whiteness."

In his 2019 review of the fiftieth anniversary edition of James Cone's *Black Theology and Black Power*, Dr. Andre Johnson Black, associate professor at the University of Memphis, enthusiastically declares,

> The 50th-anniversary edition of *Black Theology and Black Power* comes at a time in history not unlike the moment in history in which Cone originally wrote. Just a cursory examination of the six chapters in the book reads like a clarion prophetic call for us to reexamine our own theological presuppositions.... While Cone was one of the first to see a connection of religion and spirituality to Black Power, others today are making the same connection to BLM. Scholars such as Leah Gunning Francis, Elise M. Edwards, Hebah H. Farrag, and a host of pastors and religious leaders are seeing the spirituality emanating from BLM. Channeling Cone, I have publicly declared that Black Lives Matter is the gospel.

As BLM activists and black academics such as Dr. Johnson declare that "Black Lives Matter is the gospel," they understand that James Cone is the spiritual Marxist godfather of the BLM movement. In Cone's *The Black Church and Marxism*, he calls on blacks to "indigenize

Marxism, that is, to reinterpret it for our own situation … perhaps what we need today is to return to that 'good old-time religion' of our grandparents and combine it with a Marxist critique of society. Together black religion and Marxist philosophy may show us the way to build a completely new society. With that combination, we may be able to realize the freedom of which we sing and pray for in the black church."

Simply put, Black Liberation Theology is about righteous "blackness," as sinful "whiteness" can never understand blackness or how their bourgeois white privilege oppresses anyone of color. Sadly, Black Liberation Theology, which was supposed to liberate and uplift the black community, has done the opposite. Following a Marxist ideological framework leads only to more cyclical self-oppression, regression, and violence.

Dr. Anthony Bradley, a black professor of theology at King's College in New York City, states,

> Black liberation theology, originally intended to help the black community, may have actually hurt many blacks by promoting racial tension, victimology, and Marxism, which ultimately leads to more oppression. As the failed "War on Poverty" has exposed, the best way to keep the blacks perpetually enslaved to government as "daddy" is to preach victimology, Marxism, and to seduce blacks into thinking that upward mobility is someone else's responsibility in a free society.

Another Marxist "ideological framework" that BLM leadership works from is CRT or "Critical Race Theory." To understand CRT, one needs to understand cultural Marxist "Critical Theory." Many European Marxist academics during the first half of the twentieth century realized that Karl Marx's "dictatorship of the proletariat," which called for a militant international workers revolution, was not going to succeed in an overt militant manner. Far too many "workers" were moving up in society to middle-class status and were enjoying unprecedented prosperity in many liberal democracies.

A brilliant cultural Marxist was Italian Antonio Gramsci (1891–1937). He not only argued that liberal democratic economic prosperity would hinder the advancement of Marxism, but he also argued that Marx's "worker's paradise" would never be achieved as long as Christian culture shaped the worldview of the masses in Western civilization. Gramsci wrote that Western civilization had been thoroughly infused with Christianity for 2,000 years, and that as long as the Judeo-Christian worldview remained the predominant ethical, moral, and philosophical system in Europe and North America, "pure Communism" and its goal for the perfect society would never be achieved.

Gramsci observed that Christianity's cultural practices and moral persuasions were so much a part of the daily lives of nearly everyone in society, including non-Christians living in "Christian lands," that it had established an almost impossible wall for Marxists to breach to create a Marxist utopia. Therefore, in place of a militant frontal attack, Gramsci taught that with a patient evolutionary pace and not with reactionary revolutionary violence, it was much more advantageous to attack the enemy's Christian society with slow, subtle, stealth strategies. He called this cultural Marxist approach "the long march through the institutions."

Gramsci's ideas caught on like wildfire with academics throughout Europe. One such academic was Hungarian George Lukacs who, as deputy commissar for culture in Communist Hungary, declared in 1919, "Who shall save us from Western civilization?!" Lukacs' self-described "cultural terrorism" attacked Hungary's Christian mores on sex by developing an "anything goes" sex education curriculum in Hungarian schools. Unfortunately for Lukacs, Hungary's Marxist government fell as Hungarian workers and Christian traditionalists refused to accept their attempt to destroy Hungarian Christian civilization.

Lukas fled Hungary and connected with Antonio Gramsci in Vienna, Austria, where they exchanged ideas on how to further advance cultural Marxism. Out of those ideas came the Institute for Social Research in Frankfurt, Germany, which eventually became known as the Frankfurt School, modeled after the Marx-Engels Institute in Moscow. Many of the Frankfurt School academics were Jews who, as atheists, rejected biblical Judaism and Christianity.

By 1933, many of the Jewish professors of the Frankfort School, realizing that National Socialism and its Nazi adherents had no room for their brand of socialism nor their "Jewish blood," fled to America. There, they experienced profound academic freedom to promulgate their disdain for America's Judeo-Christian culture, republican form of government, and the capitalistic system.

These Frankfurt School Marxist professors landed university teaching jobs throughout the United States from

Columbia University in New York City all the way to the University of California-Berkeley. With covert calculation, they translated political Marxism into cultural Marxist terms and set about to disseminate and indoctrinate young impressionable minds throughout the 1930s, 40s, 50s, and the revolutionary 60s with neo-Marxist "Critical Theory."

Mixing cultural Marxism with the then-popular, sexually debased Freudian psychoanalysis, Critical Theory was a militant secularism based on the destructive criticism and denigration of the main elements of Western civilization: Christianity, authority, the nuclear family of a mother and father, traditional values, patriotism, sexual restraint, American republicanism, and liberal democracy.

With unrelenting criticism of every traditional and Christian institution, especially the family, the cultural Marxists hoped to not only wear down their opponents but also to have them eventually join their communist cause. Marxist Max Horkheimer taught that mankind was in a constant state of psychological repression by Christian civilization that perpetuated a monogamous, "husband and wife culture" at the expense of homosexuals and other "natural" sexual lifestyles.

Horkheimer's Frankfurt School colleague Theodor Adorno, in his 1950 book *The Authoritarian Personality*, created a Marxist construct that he called the "F-scale." Adorno's "F-scale" concluded that the traditional patriarchal family, whose values in many cases derived from Christian culture, was "F" or Fascist. Adorno said all men were fascist toward women, white men were fascist toward minorities, and it was fascist to not accept alternative sexual lifestyles such as homosexuality.

As we have learned, it is not a coincidence that on college campuses today it is fashionable for lefties, Antifa, and BLM activists to label all their ideological and political opponents as fascists. To Adorno, the Marxist call to abolish the Christian bourgeois family was the key to destroying the biggest impediment to their utopian dreams of the end of Western Christian civilization. Destroy the nuclear family, and you create the new man, the new society liberated from the oppression of bourgeois man. Remember George Lukacs' declaration, "Who shall save us from Western civilization?!" or Jesse Jackson's "Hey, Hey, Ho, Ho, Western civs got to go!"

We shouldn't be surprised that when the "trained Marxist" leadership of BLM put on their website the declaration that "We disrupt the Western-prescribed nuclear family structure.... We foster queer affirming network.... We make space for transgender brothers and sisters," they are expressing their cultural Marxist worldview. The lefty Marxist political agenda of BLM is at war with the Judeo-Christian "Adam and Eve" nuclear family. This is a family structure that black families and all families desperately need to succeed in developing the content of character and preserving the Christian civilization that Martin Luther King Jr. envisioned in his American dream.

Evolving out of this Marxist Critical Theory were various aspects of what became known as "Critical Legal Theory" and "Critical Race Theory," or CRT. This cultural Marxist "theory" was a social construct in which it was concluded that the legal structural institutions in Western society were determined by a white supremacist superstructure. This was dominated by a white society in which whites would in perpetuity keep black society and other minority societies in servitude. One of the famous originators of Critical Race Theory was Barack Obama's friend and mentor at Harvard Law School, Derrick Bell.

Dr. Bell, along with other CRT advocates, believed that the U.S. Constitution was a "capitalistic" document incapable of the redistribution of wealth and power to achieve equality for all. To create a more equal and just world, the dominant white American legal structure would have to be endlessly criticized, attacked, and torn down from within. Dr. Bell taught that "white supremacy" has so corrupted the legal system that there cannot be equal protection under the law until the system is made unequal. This would compensate for the innate racism of the white majority. CRT believes that racism cannot be ended within the current "white" system; thus, it must be transformed with black minority opinions superseding white majority opinions and law.

CRT is a profoundly disturbing Marxist theory that has at its heart the destruction of our constitutional republic and the dream of Martin Luther King Jr. Jefferey J. Pile in the *Boston College Law Review* warns us of Critical Race Theory when he writes:

> Critical race theorists attack the very foundations of classical liberal legal order, including equality theory, legal reasoning, Enlightenment rationalism and neutral principles of constitutional law. These liberal values, they allege, have no enduring

basis in principle, but are mere social constructs calculated to legitimate white supremacy. The rule of law, according to critical race theorists, is a false promise of principled government, and they have lost patience with false promises.

According to CRT, America is irredeemably racist. To quote Derrick Bell's student Barack Obama, "Racism is in our DNA," and it is inextricably woven into the fabric of America's white racist past since the first black slave arrived on American soil in 1619. The theorists believe that the July 4, 1776, clarion call of "equality for all" is a myth clocked in empty rhetoric. When President Obama was asked about the inordinate amount of tragic black-on-black murder and crime in Chicago, he said the violence is a result of "humiliation and untrammeled fury" caused not by a black criminal culture and activity, but by white systemic racism that goes back to 1619.

It is why in the midst of the George Floyd riots with its wild looting, riots, destruction of black and white businesses and property, and the harming or killing of many innocent black and white citizens, BLM leadership does not condemn their lawless actions. They believe they are participating in the breakdown of the white system that has oppressed them for 400 years. According to BLM, now is the time to burn down the system literally by any means necessary. Black Lives Matter leadership has taken the "ideological framework" of the Marxist Black Liberation movement and Marxist Black Liberation Theology to "indigenize Marxism" and the "Marxist philosophy" as a way to "build a completely new society."

One of the biggest supporters of the BLM movement
is Princeton professor Cornel West. In Dr. West's 1979
book *Black Theology and Marxist Thought,* he sees an
inextricable relationship between Marxist thought and black
theology. Both focus on the plight of the oppressed and the
exploited people of the world. This ideological commonality
sees Dr. West call for "a serious dialogue between black
theologians and Marxist thinkers ... a dialogue that centers
on the possibility of mutually arrived at political action." In
his 1991 book *The Ethical Dimensions of Marxist Thought,*
Dr. West says that Marx has been profoundly misinterpreted
by many so-called "Marxists," and that when you study Karl
Marx's thought, you find a mind dedicated to the ethical
"values of democracy, individuality, and freedom."

Dr. West sees the BLM movement as a purely peaceful
movement improperly characterized by a white supremacist
society as militant in nature. During the George Floyd BLM
protests and riots, Dr. West was one of their most vociferous
defenders. He attacked former President Obama by saying,

> It's amazing to see brother Barack Obama out there
> acting like he's part of the vanguard and struggling
> against police power when Black Lives Matter
> emerged under his administration, with his Black
> attorney general, with his Black [secretary of]
> homeland security ... but he helped militarise those
> police departments. He helped generate the levels
> of poverty when he had bailed out the Wall Street
> criminals. And we haven't gotten to the foreign
> policy yet, in terms of dropping bombs on innocent
> brothers and sisters in different parts of the world,
> especially in the Middle East and Asia. We haven't

even gotten to the killing of innocent Palestinian brothers and sisters with the U.S.-supported Israel Defense Forces.

Here we see a hardcore lefty professor, a defender of Karl Marx and BLM, viciously attack America's first black president as the "militarizer" of the police departments, killer of innocent Palestinian brothers, and supporter of Israel. Dr. West reiterates the anti-Israel, anti-police worldview of BLM, even at the expense of President Obama, "the war criminal."

In the spirit of Dr. West, even though much of the money given to BLM goes to various Democratic Party political venues, they will not hesitate to harass Democratic presidential candidates as they did with Hillary Clinton and Bernie Sanders in 2016 and again with Bolshevik Bernie in 2020. BLM co-founder Patrisse Cullors declared that we protest Democrats because Democrats have "milked the Black vote while creating policies that completely decimate Black communities." For once, I agree with Cullors. In reality, BLM works to take over the Democratic Party.

Remember when NYC BLM leader Newsome said, "If this country doesn't give us what we want, then we will burn down this system and replace it ... literally"? When you "indigenize Marxism" and the "Marxist philosophy" as a way to "build a completely new society," utilizing a Karl Marx that has a bogus love for "ethical democracy" and a Jesus who is a "black radical revolutionary," you create a radical militant movement. At the heart of this movement is the belief that it will ultimately transform and destroy the old American white supremacist republic and replace it with a Marxist revolutionary government.

With all this destructive rhetoric and actions of Antifa and the trained Marxists of BLM, we must ask ourselves this question: What is underlying this hatred of America and the Christian, liberal democratic values that made our constitutional republic a great nation that millions from around the world still desire to become a part of?

The answer, I believe, is rooted in an anti-Christian, anti-Western civilization, anti-liberal democracy culture disseminated, perpetuated, and indoctrinated by the lefty educational establishment of America, the activist media, postmodern Hollywood, and the Democratic Party. This Boomer generation American is saddened and profoundly concerned to see far too many of the Zoomer and Millennial generations join the militant pied pipers of *mobocracy*, justifying their destructive and hateful ways across the land.

All one has to do is go to the BLM website, and you will quickly realize that BLM is MUCH more than just about "police brutality and criminal justice." They are about supporting queer, LGBT, and Palestinian liberation; attacking Israel; abolishing police departments; disrupting the Western-prescribed nuclear family structure; making space for transgender brothers and sisters; and backing sundry other left-wing ideas that go way beyond a few bad police.

Let's see what many black scholars and commentators have to say about leftist and BLM claims and why, when they challenge those claims, they are derisively and viciously attacked as "Uncle Toms" and "Aunt Jemimas."

Chapter 3

Uncle Tom: Lies, Damned Lies, and Statistics

In the 1990s, liberal Harvard sociology professor Orlando Patterson wrote,

> America, while still flawed in its race relations ...
> is now the least racist white majority society in the
> world; has a better record of legal protection of
> minorities that any other society, white or black;
> and offers more opportunities to a greater number
> of black persons than any other society, including
> all those of Africa.

It is most unfortunate that when this black liberal sociologist, a writer for the *New Left Review* and a darling of Ivy League intellectuals, is attacked by his fellow lefties as an Uncle Tom, Oreo Cookie, and a traitor to the cause of civil rights and justice. Why was there such a non-intelligent visceral sophomoric reaction to the stated facts of Dr. Patterson?

It's quite simple, really. Dr. Patterson spoke profound truth into the academic body politic, challenging the victimization narrative that has been peddled routinely in academic journals and university classrooms since the 1960s. Put another way, Dr. Orlando Patterson did not kowtow to the Democratic Party line of left-wing political correctness and activist media newspeak and groupthink.

Dr. Patterson is not alone in the world of lefty "Uncle Tom" *ad hominem* and *reductio ad absurdum* rhetorical retorts. Before I go on to mention a list of famous "Uncle Toms" who dared to challenge the politically correct leftist status quo, we need to understand who Uncle Tom was and what he turned out to become. Uncle Tom was the main black character in Harriet Beecher Stowe's 1852 classic book *Uncle Tom's Cabin; or Life among the Lowly.* Uncle Tom's character is extraordinarily Christian. He daily reads his worn-out Bible, loves Jesus and all those around him, constantly reminding people of God's Kingdom above. Stowe humanizes and Christianizes the suffering of slavery for her white readers by portraying Uncle Tom as a suffering Jesus-like figure. He is ultimately beaten to death by a barbaric slave master on a small beam symbolic of a cross because he refused to give the whereabouts of two female slaves who have escaped to freedom.

Uncle Tom's Cabin became an instant bestseller, second only to the Bible in sales in the 1850s, and educated many people in the North as to the evil nature and conditions of Southern Democratic Party slavery. The Republican

Party was created two years after *Uncle Tom's* debut in 1854 in Ripon, Wisconsin, and many Republicans attribute their reading of the book as the catapult that spurred them to political action against the party of systemic institutionalized slavery—the Democratic Party.

The great black statesman and abolitionist Frederick Douglass called *Uncle Tom's Cabin* "a flash to light a million camp fires in front of the embattled hosts of slavery." The main source of Harriet Beecher Stowe's Uncle Tom was from the 1849 book, *The Life of Joshua Hensen, Formerly a Slave, Now an Inhabitant of Canada, as Narrated by Himself*. Joshua Hensen's book was a detailed description of the horrors of life in the Democratic South and his escape into freedom in the North. Hensen's story and Christian character inspired Harriet Beecher Stowe to write her classic book *Uncle Tom's Cabin*.

Unfortunately, the brave righteous Uncle Tom character as portrayed in the book in later years is not depicted as the noble honorable Christian in subsequent stage presentations. They grossly distort him into an older, illiterate, servile lackey who sells out his fellow slave brothers to gain the favor of his white master and many whites around him. This distorted negative "Uncle Tom" character was the one that drew the disdain of many black Americans and developed into a derisive term for blacks. The term has now come to represent "a black man considered excessively obedient or servile to white people" or "a person regarded as betraying their culture or social allegiance." In modern political parlance, Uncle Tom is "a black person betraying allegiance to the Democratic Party and becoming a Republican, Conservative, or Libertarian."

How ironic when you consider that the Democratic Party was the party of systemic institutionalized slavery and Jim Crow for well over 100 years of its history. The female version of Uncle Tom became "Aunt Jemima," named after the famous pancake syrup, which due to the George Floyd riots, is no longer the name of the famous syrup.

A record-breaking, very popular 2020 documentary titled *Uncle Tom*, produced and co-written by conservative radio host Larry Elder, depicts what life is like for black conservatives in America—as minorities within a minority group. Elder says the movie delivers a sharp look at "the grief that people who are black and conservative get for just saying they're not Democrats. The film really is attacking the way the Uncle Tom term is commonly used to demean people that have rethought their assumptions to the Democratic Party. I think it is in the country's best interest to disabuse blacks of the idea that they're victims and the Democratic Party deserve 95% of their vote. It is in everybody's interest to break that narrative."

The list of famous "Uncle Toms" or "Aunt Jemimas" is quite extensive and includes Supreme Court Justice Clarence Thomas; Secretary of Housing and Urban Development Ben Carson; former Secretary of State Condoleezza Rice; Senator Tim Scott of Virginia; presidential candidates Herman Cain and Alan Keyes (whom I voted for); former Congressmen Allen West, JC Watts, and Will Hurd; RNC chairman Michael Steele; professors John McWhorther, Thomas Sowell, Shelby Steele, Carol Swain, Walter Williams, Ward Connerly, Jason Hill, Ian Rowe, K Carl Smith, and Will Johnson; former National Chairman of Congress of Racial Equality Roy Innis; National Spokesperson of Congress of

Racial Equality Niger Innis; and social commentators such as Candice Owens, Starr Parker, Amy Holmes, Joseph C. Phillips, Jesse Lee Peterson, David Webb, Daneen Borelli, Burgess Owens, Larry Elder, Armstrong Williams, Deroy Murdock, Derryck Green, Sheriff David Clarke, Eric July, and Nestride Yumga; Alveda King, niece of Martin Luther King Jr.; and many, many more.

What do they all have in common besides their pigmentation and love of our American nation? It's their worldview. It's their "sin" of believing in Christian, conservative, traditional, or libertarian values that clash, challenge, and contradict the leftwing Democratic ideological worldview and the narrative of pigmentation politics and identity victimization. The victimization is eternal and is the Democratic Party's political bread and butter, the basis of their power and control in America.

During the 2019–2020 Democratic presidential debates, we heard all the candidates trashing America as a racist nation. Bernie Sanders declared America "is a racist society from top to bottom." Pete Buttigieg stated, "I am convinced that white supremacy is the force more likely to destroy the American dream." Joe Biden (poor Joe) said verbatim, "The fact is that we in fact there is systemic racism … the original sin of racism still stains our nation today." We hear the ubiquitous terms "systemic racism," "structural racism," or "institutional racism" flowing out of the mouths of Democratic politicians, BLM advocates, Antifa anarchists, lefty activist media pundits, and Hollywood Neanderthals daily.

In response to the BLM and Antifa George Floyd rioting, a classic activist media perspective is perfectly illustrated with the June 8, 2020, *Washington Post* headline that declared, "Trump Republican Party Displays Its Systemic Racism." The term "systemic racism" or "institutional racism" was popularized by the civil rights activist and Black Panther Marxist Stokely Carmichael in his 1967 book *Black Power: The Politics of Liberation.*

The left-wing Washington D.C. Urban Institute, founded by Democratic President Lyndon B. Johnson in 1968, defines institutional or "structural racism" this way:

> Throughout this country's history, the hallmarks of American democracy—opportunity, freedom, and prosperity—have been largely reserved for white people through the intentional exclusion and oppression of people of color. The deep racial and ethnic inequities that exist today are a direct result of structural racism: the historical and contemporary policies, practices, and norms that create and maintain white supremacy.

As time went on in the 1960s, "Black Power" advocate Stokely Carmichael grew more and more frustrated with the power of white supremacy that permeated the structures, systems, and institutions of the white-dominated American society. He also became disillusioned in his work with SNCC (Student Nonviolent Coordinating Committee) and the slow pacifist approach of Martin Luther King's SCLC (Southern Christian Leadership Conference).

Carmichael was profoundly influenced by Marxist writer Franz Fanon's *Wretched of the Earth.* Fanon argues in his chapter "On Violence" that the dominant white supremacist ideology of the colonial ruling class could be destroyed only through violent means to achieve the necessary end of "black liberation." Carmichael transformed Fanon's Marxist analysis into black American terms when he rejected the slow liberal non-violent SNCC and SCLC's desire to assimilate into "white middle class existence."

Black liberation, according to Carmichael, must be established outside the oppressive white power structure that was systemic and permeated with "colonial" institutional racism, replacing the "Freedom now!" slogan of non-violent advocate Martin Luther King Jr. with "Black Power!" Carmichael declared in his 1967 book *Black Power: The Politics of Liberation,* "a 'nonviolent' approach to civil rights is an approach black people cannot afford and a luxury white people do not deserve."

In a May 1967 London speech at a Marxist Dialectics Liberation Conference, Carmichael declared that black people were fighting against "a system of international white supremacy coupled with internationalism capitalism."

Marxist Stokely Carmichael was an admirer and friend of Communist Fidel Castro, who hated "international capitalism" and wanted to destroy the United States with nuclear bombs. Marxist Dictator Fidel Castro died November 25, 2016. On November 27, 2016, the Black Lives Matter Global Network website put out an article titled, "Lessons from Fidel: Black Lives Matter and the Transition of El Comandante." Here is what BLM wrote:

> We are feeling many things as we awaken
> to a world without Fidel Castro. There is an

overwhelming sense of loss, complicated by fear
and anxiety. Although no leader is without flaws,
we must push back against the rhetoric of the right
and come to the defense of El Comandante.... As
a Black network committed to transformation, we
are particularly grateful to Fidel for holding Mama
Assata Shakur, who continues to inspire us. We
are thankful that he provided a home for Brother
Michael Finney Ralph Goodwin, and Charles Hill,
asylum to Brother Huey P. Newton, and sanctuary
for so many other Black Revolutionaries who were
being persecuted by the American government
during the Black Power era.... As Fidel ascends
to the realm of the ancestors, we summon his
guidance, strength, and power as we recommit
ourselves to the struggle for universal freedom.
Fidel Vive!

Notice BLM's reference to the "Black Power era" and
those individuals whom Castro protected from American
justice. Brothers Michael Finney, Ralph Goodwin, and
Charles Hill were members of the black militant group the
Republic of New Afrika. You may remember the Marxist
Harry Haywood's 1930s call for the creation of a separate
black country within the United States. In the 1960s, a
Communist organization, RAM (Revolutionary Action
Movement), which mixed the ideas of Marx, Lenin, Mao,
and Malcolm X, called for the resurrection of Haywood's
vision of a "black nation," the Republic of New Afrika, which
was to be composed of the American states of Alabama,
Georgia, Louisiana, Mississippi, South Carolina, and the
black majority counties surrounding the area of Arkansas,
Florida, North Carolina, Tennessee, and Texas.

The three Marxist comrades Finney, Goodwin, and Hill stole a car in 1971 in Albuquerque, New Mexico. When apprehended, they killed Officer Robert Rosenbloom. They escaped justice by hijacking TWA Flight 106 with 49 people on board at Albuquerque Airport. They demanded $200,000 and to be flown to Communist Cuba. Their demands were met. These were the comrades who were provided homes by Castro, sparking thankfulness by BLM.

Who is "Brother Huey P. Newton"? Newton was the co-founder of the Marxist Black Panther Party in 1966. In October 1967, Newton allegedly shot and killed a police officer during a traffic stop and was charged with manslaughter. He was later acquitted by the "racist" system. Years later, he was charged with the murder of Kathleen Smith, and after bail he fled to Cuba. He came back to the U.S., and after two trials, the "racist" system acquitted him again. In 1970, after his release from prison, Newton visited Communist China and was treated as a "Marxist" hero, visiting delegates from Communist North Korea and Communist Vietnam. In his 1973 autobiography *Revolutionary Suicide*, Newton praised Communist North Korea and Vietnam and called Communist China "a free and liberated territory with a socialist government."

Let us not forget how the BLM eulogy to Comrade Castro was "particularly grateful to Fidel for holding Mama Assata Shakur," the cop killer militant Marxist of Black Liberation Army fame and hero to many within the BLM movement. It is obvious that the godfather of BLM, Marxist Stokely Carmichael, and his comrade Marxist Fidel Castro profoundly helped shape the Marxist worldview of Black

Lives Matter whose ultimate goal is the destruction of "white capitalism."

Disillusioned with white activists working within the Black Panther Party, Stokely Carmichael moved to Guinea in 1969 and changed his name to Kwame Ture. Carmichael/Ture spent the last thirty years of his life dedicated to the principles of A-APRP (All-African People's Revolutionary Party), whose 2020 website declares, "[A-APRP] will at the same time advance the triumph of the international socialist revolution, and the onward progress towards world communism, under which, every society is ordered the principle of—from each according to his ability, to each according to his needs." This Marxist declaration of "progress toward world communism" is the manifesto of Black Lives Matter leadership from top to bottom.

The same year Carmichael defined "institutional racism" in 1967, he was shattered by the death of his hero, the famous Argentinean Communist Che Guevara. Carmichael lamented, "The death of Che Guevara places a responsibility on all revolutionaries of the World to redouble their decision to fight on to the final defeat of imperialism. That is why in essence Che Guevara is not dead; his ideas are with us."

It is quite true that the ideas of Marxists Che Guevera and Stokely Carmichael are not dead but are with us. In fact, they are alive and well in the heart of BLM Marxist ideology and actions as they, along with leftist Democratic leaders, declare that systemic, institutional, and structural racism is alive and well in the white racist nation of the United States of America.

According to this modern-day leftist Black Power BLM narrative, slavery and systemic racism are our "original sins." These sins go back to 1619 and cannot be forgiven or redeemed. They must be perpetually held before us as an eternal reminder of who whites are and what they can never become.

Free from white guilt, white privilege, and whiteness daily puts whites in the dock of judgment before a BLM tribunal that demands reparations for slavery, free health care, free college education for the oppressed, free Palestine, elimination of the police and the criminal justice system, mandated lefty indoctrination re-education camps, and the prostrating/taking of a knee before the BLM lords and priggish pompous white leftists.

Before we analyze the charge of the so-called institutional racist American society from "top to bottom," I ask this question: If we are one of the most oppressive and racist nations in the world according to Antifa, BLM, and the Democratic Party, why do many black scholars such as John McWhorter in 2020 conclude that "America has never been less racist" and Orlando Patterson in the 1990s declare that "America is now the least racist white majority society in the world" and "offers more opportunities to greater number of black persons than any other society including all of Africa"?

Can Dr. Patterson's claims be substantiated? Yes, they can!

According to the Pew Research Center, "Significant voluntary black migration is a relatively new development—and one that has increased rapidly over the past two decades."

The Pew Research Center states: "The black immigration population has increased five fold since 1980. There were 4.2 million black immigrants living in the U.S. in 2016, up from 816,000 in 1980.... Since 2000 alone the number of black immigrants living in the country has risen 71%. Now roughly, one in ten blacks (9%) living in the U.S. are foreign born, up from 3% in 1980."

The Pew Research Center goes on to say, "Much of the recent growth in foreign born-black population has been fueled by African migration. Between 2000 and 2016, the black African immigration population more than doubled from 574,000 to 1.6 million. Africans now make up 39% of the overall foreign born black population, up from 24% in 2000. Still, roughly half of all foreign born blacks living in the U.S. in 2016 (49%) were from the Caribbean, with Jamaica and Haiti being the largest source countries."

If, according to the Democratic Party and BLM, America is such an egregious racist, imperialistic, white supremacist nation, why has there been such an explosion of black immigration in the past few decades to the U.S.? Why do the overwhelming majority of those African and black Caribbean immigrants become lovers of America and passionate U.S. citizens who reject the lefty narrative of systemic racism from top to bottom?

Many black and white scholars are convinced it's because they have not been indoctrinated by an American education system dominated by lefty academics and lefty activist media pundits whose agenda is to sell the myth of perpetual systemic racism.

Dr. Jason D. Hill, a black Jamaican-American professor of philosophy at DePaul University in Chicago, another one of those "Uncle Toms," tells us in his book *We Have Overcome: A Immigrants Letter to the American People* that the controlling lefty narrative repeated by the activist media and from the angry words of Democratic political activists is the bipolar opposite of how American society really is.

Hill writes that they paint a portrait of an America permeated with white supremacy privilege where blacks/minorities are locked in poverty worse than slavery. Dr. Hill corrects this false narrative by telling us he came to America at the age of twenty from Jamaica and did not find intractable institutional racism. Instead, he found a constitutional republic full of plentiful opportunity, a country where he could get a college education and eventually become a professor at a renowned American university.

Professor Hill goes on to explain it wasn't white systemic racism that sought to keep him down but the constant nay-saying negative narrative from the left and organizations such as BLM that denigrated him because he did not embrace their Marxist ideology of victimization, where "bourgeois" white man dominates the "proletariat" black man.

I quote Dr. Hill extensively from an excellent June 2018 article for *Commentary* magazine titled "My 'Black Lives Matter' Problem." Dr. Hill writes:

> When some black folks complain that white people don't value black lives, I often ask: What exactly do you mean? In fact, too many black Americans are

reluctant to hold other black people accountable
for the horrific crimes they are committing against
one another. Members of Black Lives Matter want
white people to esteem black lives and value the
humanity of black people when they themselves
can't condemn and express moral outrage at those
who maim and kill black children in the course of
gang warfare, senseless street violence, and drive-
by shootings. Why do white people have a larger
moral responsibility to care about black people
than black people have to care about their own
lives? And why are blacks in need of special white
nurturance?

Compared with the recent spate of police killings
of unarmed black men, black-on-black crime
is tantamount to a national-security disaster.
The moral hysteria raised by a few incidents of
police brutality in the face of this larger national
tragedy is reckless hyperbole. It hides from the
nation a deep malaise at work in the psyche of
some in the black community: a form of self-
hatred that manifests itself in a homicidal rage not
fundamentally against white people, but against
other black people.

Dr. Hill also exposes the intense anti-Israel ideology of BLM
when he brilliantly writes:

The leaders of Black Lives Matter have written
a profoundly anti-Israel (and anti-American)
manifesto in which they accuse Israel of "genocide"
and "apartheid." The manifesto endorses the

"Boycott, Divestment, Sanctions" (BDS) movement and takes the view that the United States justifies and advances the global war on terror via its alliances with Israel. This, according to Black Lives Matter, makes the U.S. complicit in a supposedly genocidal massacre of the Palestinian people. As a staunch defender of Israel on moral grounds, I categorically condemn the moral ineptitude of the Black Lives Matter movement on this point. If there is a victim in the Middle East, it is the beleaguered state of Israel.

Another black immigrant from Cameroon, Africa, Nestride Yumga moved to the United States in 2016. Yumga had been told that America was a land of deep-rooted racism that permeated the major institutions and laws in our republic. Like Jason Hill from Jamaica, Nestride Yumba from Cameroon found a land of bountiful opportunity full of incredible diversity, prosperity, liberty, and tolerance. She immediately fell in love with America and did not buy BLM's cynical narrative of a suppressive white privileged hierarchy that dominated black Americans.

During the May 31, 2020, George Floyd protests and riots in Washington D.C., Yumga, a D.C. resident, confronted the black and white lefty protestors by shouting out,

> Black Lives Matter is a joke! You are the racists! Go to Chicago. They don't have schools there and they die every day. They don't care [about you] because you can't get attention with that.... Hypocrites! Go to southeast Washington, to the northeast and tell them, "Black Lives Matter." If they matter,

they should matter everywhere. Black lives should matter everywhere. It doesn't take a white cop to kill a black man to make it matter.

Yumba was making a reference to the dramatic increase in the Washington D.C. homicide rate—a ten-year high—with the overwhelming majority being black-on-black murders.

When Yumba cried out, "Go to Chicago … they die every day," she was reflecting a horrible crime spree that was occurring as she spoke on May 31, 2020, which saw 18 people killed, making it the single most violent day in Chicago in sixty years. By Monday, June 1, 2020, 25 people were murdered and 85 were wounded. Of those homicides, 95 percent were black-on-black murder. On Father's Day weekend, June 20–22, 2020, 104 Chicagoans were shot and 14 were killed, including 5 children. One of the children was three-year-old Mekay James. Sadly, once again, it was black-on-black homicide.

When Yumba was asked about her protesting the BLM protest in D.C., she said, "I'm here because I heard about a demonstration on the George Floyd situation. I'll be honest: it's wrong for something like that to happen," she said of the George Floyd's death at the hands of an incompetent Minneapolis policeman. But Yumba added, "The problem is that it shouldn't be an opportunity for a group of people to use it as an excuse to present themselves as victims. Nobody is a victim here. The only victim here is George Floyd—let's be clear."

In a June 8, 2020, *Wall Street Journal* op-ed piece, Nestride Yumba wrote:

I am not oppressed. I am free. African-Americans need real policy reforms, not racial antagonism.... America has a major problem called *violence*. The high crime rates in African-American communities demand more social activism and economic initiatives in recognition of the value of all black lives. But the Black Lives Matter movement throws racial antagonism into this equation to create an even bigger problem by turning Americans against each other, tearing down our cities, and bringing shame and disgrace to our great country. Black Lives Matter and its supporters don't represent all black Americans. They don't represent our communities, they don't speak for us, they don't act in our best interests, and they don't care about our prosperity. The overwhelming majority of black Americans are for peaceful, effective protests, like those led by Martin Luther King, and for real reforms that help us prosper and be free.

During the George Floyd riots of late May 2020 in New York City, BLM activists went beyond peaceful protesting and began looting, burning cop cars, and destroying businesses. In a heartbreaking video posted on social media, an elderly black woman yelled at the BLM looters who destroyed her business.

"Look what you did to my store. Look!" she said, pointing behind her at an exposed storefront with wires hanging from the ceiling and people cleaning up inside. "Look what you did to my store! Look at the things you've done. Look. We've been here all night cleaning up. All night cleaning. Tell me Black Lives Matter. You lied. You wanted to loot the store. You needed money? Get a job—like I do. Stop stealing. This is a neighborhood. We're trying to build it up and you're tearing it down!"

"You're tearing it down!" Remember the words of NYC BLM leader Hawk Newsome who declared during a Fox News interview: "If this country doesn't give us what we want, then we will burn down this system and replace it!"

BLM wants the American system replaced with a Marxist one.

So while the BLM leadership calls for revenging and dismantling police departments across America, where is their outrage and nationwide protesting for the death of innocent three-year-old MeKay James and the thousands of blacks killed by other blacks every year?!

Where are the Democratic Party–BLM college scholarships, streets, memorials, ceremonies named and performed after MeKay James?! There are none, and we know why. MeKay James does not fit the white supremacy systematic black victimization narrative pushed by left-wing academics and Marxist revolutionaries.

For many years now, "Uncle Tom" black scholars have explained that the systemic scenario pushed by the left is not true. Black American Dr. Shelby Steele, author of *Content of Our Character: A New Vision of Race in America*, writes, "Instead of admitting that racism has declined, we [blacks] argue all the harder that it is still alive and more insidious than ever. We hold race up to shield us from what we do not want to see in ourselves." BLM does not want us to see the following names:

Jaquawn Newman, 26; Joseph Brooks, 34; Jalieel
Jackson, 28; Lazarra Daniels,18;Tommie Gatewood
Jr., 27; Kenneth McKinney, 53; Andrew Crues,
34; Tyrel Clark, 25; David Green, 39; Lenell
McClain, 26; Shanon Stewart, 24; Ricky Hulitt, 36;
John Tiggs, 32; Larita Kinley, 37; Alex Clark, 21;
Gerald Johnson Jr., 31; Andre Jackson, 24; Loren
Johnson, 42; Remone Butler, 27; Dante Denny,
29; Johnathan Stanton, 31; Pierre Johnson, 30;
Keenan Lee, 35; Randle Lee, 41; James Barnes,
24; Antonio Gasaway, 35; Mylonia Winbush, 30;
Dariontae Adams, 21; Johnny Cox, 36; Safarian
Herring, 26; Darius Ross, 30; Courtney Horton,
32; Anthony McMillen, 26; Kevin Applewhite, 35;
Victor Hudson, 30; Denzail Gresham, 27; Robert
Chitty, 49; Robert Owens, 31; Dannarius Lipscomb,
41; Dennis Paige, 27; Tomarri Johnson, 19; Tyrone
Thomas, 19; Cincere Joiner, 17; Jeremiah James,
15; Jazzlyn Robison, 15; Keishanay Bolden, 18; and
McKay James, 3.

The list could go on and on and on. What do all these
names have in common? They were killed—murdered in the
Chicago area in late May or early June of 2020 as the BLM
George Floyd protests and riots were happening all across
America. They are all black victims who were murdered by
black criminals.

Eighteen-year-old Keishanay Bolden was shot in the
torso during an argument with a black male suspect in
West Englewood. She was a student at Western Illinois
University, an inspiring lawyer majoring in law enforcement
and justice administration. She had just recently written

a paper about black gun violence in her neighborhood. You didn't hear much about Keishanay and the hundreds of black victims of crime by blacks in the Democratic-controlled cities of Chicago, St. Louis, Milwaukee, Philadelphia, New York, Baltimore, Detroit, Minneapolis, Cleveland, Pittsburgh, Oakland, Newark, Memphis, and many other urban centers. I wonder why. I wonder what Keishanay was learning and would have learned in her law enforcement classes at WIU.

Would she have learned that hundreds of black Americans were murdered in 2019, and that 2020 appears to be no different? Would she have learned that, well over 90 percent of the time, the murderers were also black? BLM social justice activists and leftists love to tell the world that what blacks have to fear most is being shot at and killed by the police. Would Keishanay have learned that the BLM-leftist narrative claiming an epidemic of white racists cops killing black suspects just isn't so and the numbers don't add up?

Since 2015, the *Washington Post* (not a friend to conservatives) has created a database cataloging every fatal shooting. In 2019, 1,004 people were shot and killed by police. Blacks, who comprise 13.4% of the U.S. population, were about 25% of those killed by police. That percentage of black victims is significantly lower than what the black crime rate would potentially predict. The 2018 data show that blacks made up 53% of known murder offenders and commit about 60% of robberies in the U.S.

Heather MacDonald, the author of *The War on Cops: How the New Attack on Law and Order Makes Everyone Less Safe*, writes:

The police fatally shot 9 unarmed blacks and 19 unarmed whites in 2019, according to a *Washington Post* database, down from 38 and 32, respectively, in 2015. The *Post* defines "unarmed" broadly to include such cases as a suspect in Newark, N.J., who had a loaded handgun in his car during a police chase. In 2018 there were 7,407 black homicide victims. Assuming a comparable number of victims last year, those nine unarmed black victims of police shootings represent 0.1% of all African-Americans killed in 2019. By contrast, a police officer is 18½ times more likely to be killed by a black male than an unarmed black male is to be killed by a police officer.

In August 2019, in the *Proceedings of the National Academy of Science*, researchers found that the more frequently police encountered violent suspects from any given racial group, the greater chance that a member of that racial group will be fatally shot by a cop. They concluded that there is "no significant evidence of anti-black disparity in the likelihood of being fatally shot by police." The youngest tenured black American professor at Harvard, Roland G. Fryer Jr., in his *An Empirical Analysis of Racial Differences in Police Use of Force*, concluded that there was no evidence for racial discrimination in shootings. Recent studies find no institutionalized abuse of black suspects by the police; on the contrary, police officers are more reluctant and hesitant to use deadly force against a black suspect versus a white suspect.

What happened in Minneapolis to George Floyd was absolutely deplorable and horrible and an indictment on a

few bad Minneapolis cops, but it does not mean that there
is a plague of systemic racism within the Minneapolis Police
Department, or for that matter, in police departments
across America. The chief of police of Minneapolis is
Medaria Arradondo, who is black. The district's U.S.
Congressional representative is black. The state attorney
general is black. The mayor is a progressive liberal. The vice
president of the city council is black. Minneapolis is not the
Democrat Jim Crow of the 1950s Birmingham, Alabama,
and its police chief is not the infamous redneck Chief of
Police Bull Connor.

The days of Democratic systemic racism are over in
America, unless, of course, we see what is happening
with all the riots, violence, and killings in the Democrat-
controlled cities as a systemic Democratic Party policy
problem that still plagues America. I do.

The last time Baltimore, Maryland, had a Republican
mayor was in 1967. It is a profoundly Democratic-run city.
In 2015, Freddie Gray died in police custody. Of the six
officers involved in the arrest, three were black. The mayor
was a black female. The city council was majority black. The
top two officials in the Baltimore police department were
black. The state attorney who brought the charges against
the six officers was black. The judge before whom two of
the charged officers appeared was black. The U.S. attorney
general was black, as was the president of the United
States. Yes, there were negligent officers, but there was no
institutional racism, unless, of course, you put the blame on
Democratic Party policies.

We are told today that there is something in America called the "Ferguson effect," in which more and more police officers—black, brown, Asian, and white—are backing off law enforcement in minority neighborhoods due to fear of being falsely accused of systemic racism for doing their jobs. What is "Ferguson," and why has its "effect" affected American society?

On August 9, 2014, Michael Brown Jr., an 18-year-old black man, was fatally shot by a 28-year-old white Ferguson, Missouri, Police Officer Darren Wilson. The original narrative of the event spun by the activist media was that the white Officer Wilson stopped the black teenager Michael Brown for no good reason. During the altercation, Michael Brown's back was turned to Officer Wilson when he was shot and killed. Before this happened, Mr. Brown reportedly raised his hands above his head and shouted, "Hands up. Don't shoot!"

Stripped of the political and emotional narrative of lies and misinformation, a local grand jury investigation and a federal investigation both concluded that Officer Wilson was justified in his use of force. They tell a more revealing and accurate story of what actually happened on August 9, 2014, in Ferguson, Missouri.

On August 20, 2104, a St. Louis County grand jury started hearing evidence in the case of *State of Missouri v. Darren Wilson* to determine whether there was probable cause to believe Officer Wilson committed a crime against Michael Brown. The jury was selected from a randomly chosen master jury list. This Missouri grand jury consisted of three blacks (two women and one man) and nine white jurors (three women and six men) who reflected the racial demographic of St. Louis County, which is approximately 70% white and 30% black. After 25 days of listening to 60 witnesses and 5,000 pages of testimony with a preponderance of forensic evidence from powder burns, DNA, blood, shell casings, and bullet trajectory along with profound witness testimony, they concluded they could not charge Officer Wilson with a crime against Michael Brown.

Here's how the actual event occurred. Officer Wilson did stop Michael Brown for a good reason. Wilson received a call that a local convenience store had been robbed. Wilson saw two men walking near the robbed convenience store who met the description of the store thieves. Wilson approached them and asked the two men to move to the sidewalk, but Michael Brown refused. Officer Wilson then attempted to get out of his car, but Brown blocked the door and punched Wilson through the window. Then as Brown tried to take Wilson's gun, they struggled and Wilson managed to fire his gun, hitting Brown in the hand. After being shot in the hand, Brown ran away from the police car. Officer Wilson got out of the vehicle and pursued him. Brown then suddenly turned and charged Wilson. Many of the 60 witnesses, who were black, corroborated the forensic evidence when they described what happened.

One witness described it this way:

> Brown ran towards the officer full charge. The officer fired several shots at him, and Mike Brown continuously came forward in the charging motion. And when he stopped, that's when the officer ceased fire. When he charged once more, the officer

returned fire with, I would say, three to four shots. And that's when Mike Brown finally collapsed.

The Brown family's own medical forensic expert, Dr. Michael Baden, said the wounds Brown suffered were consistent with someone running toward Wilson, not running away.

Here is where BLM and the activist media used a lie for propaganda purposes to advance a radical political agenda. They made signs at the Ferguson protest and riots declaring, "Hands up. Don't shoot!" According to BLM and the lefty media, before Michael Brown was shot and killed by Officer Wilson, he raised his hands above his head and yelled out, "Hands up. Don't shoot!"

Federal investigators, many of whom were black, from the Department of Justice headed by black Attorney General Eric Holder, who was appointment by black President Barack Obama, concluded that there was "no credible evidence that Brown ever raised his hands in a 'don't shoot' gesture or in any way heeded Officer Wilson's commands for him to surrender." The federal investigation reported, "Witnesses who originally stated [on CNN, of course] Brown had his hands up in surrender recanted their original recounts, admitting they did not witness the shooting or parts of it." Witnesses recanted when they realized their lies were being contradicted by the overwhelming majority of witnesses who said it never happened, corroborating the forensics evidence.

The federal investigators also concluded, "The media has widely reported that there is witness testimony that Brown said, 'Don't shoot' as he held his hands above his head. In fact, their investigation did not reveal any eyewitnesses who stated that Brown said, 'Don't shoot.'" Where did this phrase "Hands up, don't shoot!" come from? It appears that it was made up by the other man with Michael Brown, Dorain Johnson, who after the shooting said, "The police shot my friend and his hands were up," and within a few days it became the phrase, "Hands up, don't shoot." Eventually, it was picked up by the activist media and BLM as an anthem for protestors. Both the St. Louis County grand jury and the federal investigation concluded the phrase never happened and Officer Wilson did nothing wrong. There was no evidence to prosecute him.

In her book *The War on Cops*, Heather MacDonald states, "It was not a question of evidence 'not supporting' high threshold civil rights charges; it was a question of evidence eviscerating virtually every aspect of the pro-Brown, anti-Wilson narrative." In other words, the overwhelming evidence by two investigations (with many blacks involved in the process) destroyed, to quote the *Washington Post,* the "lie of 'hands up, don't shoot'" and the major premise of Black Lives Matter and media activists that a racist white cop killed an innocent black man.

If it isn't white supremacy/systemic institutionalized racism that is causing serious social problems in black communities, then what is it? White Democratic systemic racism, which plagued America for well over 150 years, has been eliminated from American society since the Federal Civil Rights Acts of the 1960s. In the vast overwhelmingly Democratic-controlled cities in America today, the Democratic welfare state of the 1960s has not solved the serious social and economic problems of black inner city ghetto existence; in fact, it has exacerbated the problem.

Black American Bob Woodson, campaign advisor to President George W. Bush and founder of the 1776 Project, spoke on Mark Levin's July 6, 2020, *Life & Liberty* program. He stated:

> When the poverty programs came, I knew that this was a scam. See, in 1960, when the government started spending $22 trillion, 70 cents of every dollar did not go to the poor; it went to those who served the poor. They asked not which problems are solvable, but which ones are fundable.

> And so what happened is we've created a commodity out of poor people. And so, as a consequence, there were no incentives to solve problems of the poor because the careers of those serving them were dependent upon having people to serve. And that's why in the black community, you've seen the families disintegrate over the last 50 years; a hundred years prior to that, black families were intact. We have a whole history of a hundred years when black families left slavery, 80 percent of all those black families had a man and a woman raising children. And this family composition continued generation after generation.

> But in the '60s, that changed because of government policies. There was a deliberate attempt on the part of Cloward and Piven at the university—Columbia University. They said one of the ways that we can emphasize the contradictions

of capitalism is to separate work from income.
It will make the father redundant. And so that's
what the poverty programs and welfare programs
did, separate wealth from income. Make the
father redundant. And so, the nuclear family was
redefined as Eurocentric, and therefore irrelevant.
Christian faith was demeaned. And so you had
this common—government programs began to
attack the stigma that was present in the black
community on receiving welfare … so social
policies of the '60s did what racism couldn't have
accomplished before.

The black libertarian professor of economics at George
Mason University, Walter Williams, writes:

Some of the most dangerous big cities are St.
Louis, Detroit, Baltimore, Oakland, Chicago,
Memphis, Atlanta, Birmingham, Newark, Buffalo
and Philadelphia. The most common characteristic
of these cities is that for decades, all of them have
been run by liberal Democrats. Some cities—such
as Detroit, Buffalo, Newark and Philadelphia—
haven't elected a Republican mayor for more than
a half-century. On top of this, in many of these
cities, blacks are mayors, often they dominate
city councils and they are chiefs of police and
superintendents of schools.

In the 1950s there was very little black political power
in America, especially in the Democratic South. Today,
black political power has profoundly expanded as black
Americans have significant political power at all levels

of government. And yet, Democratic-controlled cities
with large sums of money procured through Democratic-
controlled teachers unions have some of the poorest quality
public education.

Why is it that once prosperous cities such as Baltimore,
Detroit, St. Louis, Cleveland, and Pittsburgh have seen
not only "white flight"—blamed by Democrats, civil rights
leaders, and academics on racism—but also "black flight"
from these Democratic-controlled cities? Why are black
Americans fleeing to "white" suburbs in Atlanta, Dallas,
Houston, Miami, Phoenix, and many other cities? White
Democrat lefties, black Democrat politicians, and BLM
activists all like to say it is because of white institutional
racism, but the answer is crime and culture.

This is perfectly explained by one of the most brilliant
academic minds in America, Thomas Sowell, a black
professor of economics and social theory at Stanford
University. Dr. Sowell states,

> That vision is nowhere more clearly expressed
> than in attempts to automatically depict whatever
> social problems exist in ghetto communities as
> being caused by the sins or negligence of whites,
> whether racism in general or a "legacy of slavery"
> in particular. Like most emotionally powerful
> visions, it is seldom, if ever, subjected to the test
> of evidence. The "legacy of slavery" argument is
> not just an excuse for inexcusable behavior in
> the ghettos. In a larger sense, it is an evasion of
> responsibility for the disastrous consequences of
> the prevailing social vision of our times, and the

political policies based on that vision, over the past half century. Anyone who is serious about evidence need only compare black communities as they evolved in the first 100 years after slavery with black communities as they evolved in the first 50 years after the explosive growth of the welfare state, beginning in the 1960s.

You would be hard-pressed to find as many ghetto riots prior to the 1960s as we have seen just in the past year, much less in the 50 years since a wave of such riots swept across the country in 1965. We are told that such riots are a result of black poverty and white racism. But in fact—for those who still have some respect for facts—black poverty was far worse, and white racism was far worse, prior to 1960. But violent crime within black ghettos was far less.

Notice some of the key points the brilliant Thomas Sowell makes.

Sowell argues that the "legacy of slavery" is not only an excuse for inexcusable behavior in the black ghettos, but is also used to feed into the Democratic welfare society of the 1960s. Studies have shown that black communities after slavery and up until the welfare state of the 1960s did not see the maladjusted behavioral problems as experience in the past 50 years.

Today's BLM riots, we are told, are due to white racism and black poverty, and yet white racism and black poverty were far worse before 1960, with violent crime in black ghettos far less. Murder rates were going down before the 1960s.

Black children had two-parent families prior to the 1960s. Today, 70 percent of black children are raised in one-parent homes. Despite the brave efforts that single black mothers demonstrate in raising their children, it's next to impossible to be both a good mother and father.

The director of the National Marriage Project, W. Bradford Wilcox, says social research shows the profoundly "negative psychological and social effects of fatherlessness on black boys." The research shows that young black boys have numerous behavioral problems that lead to criminal behavior as teenagers and adults. BLM leadership teaches that the idea of a two-parent home with a father and mother is a "white Western racist construct" that should be rejected. Is it no wonder, then, that during the George Floyd riots, many young fatherless black men became wildly violent and were beating, looting, and even killing black policemen and destroying black businesses in their attempt to "burn down the system"?

An excellent teaching tool I have used for almost thirty years is the classic 1991 film *Boyz n the Hood* by black film director John Singleton. The film was declared "culturally, historically and aesthetically significant" by the U.S. Library of Congress and is preserved in the National Film Registry. *Boyz n the Hood* is the story of a young black man, Tyr Styles, who was being raised by a single mother, Reva, in Los Angeles. Tyr's mother realizes that her son has no respect for authority. He also has a volatile temper and needs loving discipline and a positive "father culture" in his life. She has him live with his father to help him stay away from becoming a violent "gangbanger." In the end, Tyr grows up, accepts his responsibilities as a man, and does not become another victim and victimizer of a "boy n the hood." Tyr goes off to an all-black college—Moorhouse in Atlanta, Georgia—and becomes an outstanding member of American society. Director John Singleton's goal in his creative story was to show black and all communities across America the need for both fathers and mothers to instill in their children a positive content of character so desperately needed in all homes, regardless of color.

The black American family was stronger with fewer social problems in the first hundred years after slavery than since the creation of LBJ's so-called "Great Society" in the 1960s. Dr. Sowell reminds us that these "welfare state" criminal trends since the 1960s do not affect just black communities but white communities, as well. Dr. Thomas Sowell, a student of Dr. Martin Luther King Jr., becomes profoundly "Martin Luther King-esque" when he states that "behavior matters and facts matter, more than the prevailing social visions or political empires built on those visions."

Content of character and behavior matter more than the slogan "Black Lives Matter."

The BLM and leftist culture and behavior do not have an attitude of healing and bringing America together with malice toward none. Their Marxist culture of pigmentation politics includes separatism, victimology, oppression, and denial of empirical evidence. Many within the black community are thus crippled from facing the ugly reality of the criminal culture that plagues many major black urban centers across America.

When I saw leftists and BLM rioters desecrate the memorial to Robert Gould Shaw and the Massachusetts Fifty-Fourth

Regiment, I was not only disgusted by such wanton acts of violence, stupidity, and disrespect for those who sacrificed to end Democrat slavery, but I was also reminded of a scene in the movie *Glory* about the black 54th Regiment of Massachusetts. The scene illustrates the importance of civilized Christian culture that shapes behavior and the content of one's character.

In the film, white Yankee Colonel Robert Shaw, a good Christian citizen of Massachusetts—a state with a long history of fighting to end slavery going back to John Adams and John Quincy Adams—is given the command of one of the first all-black regiments in the Union Army during the Civil War. Shaw's primary duty is to train raw black recruits in the art of chivalrous warfare.

Training is described in the dictionary as "the action of teaching a person a particular skill or type of behavior." Culture is defined as the "social behavior ... of a particular group ... a cultural norm codifies acceptable conduct in society and serves as a guideline for behavior, dress, language, and demeanor in a situation." Once the 54th Massachusetts Regiment completes its training—"cultural teaching" by Colonel Robert Shaw and his officers—they are transferred to join Colonel James Montgomery and his black regiment, the 2nd South Carolina Volunteer Infantry Regiment, which has been trained in a culture of looting and pillaging.

Colonel Montgomery orders both black regiments to loot and burn down the undefended and surrendered town of Darien, Georgia. As the looting, beatings, and burning begin by the blacks of the 2nd South Carolina Regiment, the blacks of the 54th Massachusetts are shocked. Along with Colonel Shaw, they refuse to join in the looting, burning, and beating of the innocent children and women of Darien, Georgia. You can see the moral disgust on the faces of the blacks and whites of the 54th Massachusetts toward the order while the "culture" of Colonel Montgomery and the 2nd South Carolina was enjoying the looting and killing.

I have used the movie *Glory* for over 30 years in my high school and college U.S. history classes. That scene has generated some great discussions on Martin Luther King's dream of being judged by the actions and content of character created by a culture of civilization, decency, and Christian virtues versus a culture of disrespect, destruction, and death. My students see two groups or regiments of blacks acting very differently, and it has nothing to do with the pigmentation of their skin but everything to do with the values that had been inculcated into their character. Throughout history, we see that good culture equates to good character and actions, while bad culture equates to bad character and actions.

Remember how the definition of "culture" is "a cultural norm that codifies acceptable conduct in society and serves as a guideline for behavior, dress, language, and demeanor in a situation"? I want to revisit the 1960s civil rights activist Barbara Ann Reynolds' spot-on assessment of the Black Lives Matter movement today in relation to training, culture, and a proper education in civil disobedience and the just defense of civil rights in America. She states:

> In the 1960s activists confronted white mobs
> and police with dignity and decorum, sometimes

dressing in church clothes and kneeling in prayer during protests to make a clear distinction between who was evil and who was good. But at protests today, it is difficult to distinguish legitimate activists from the mob actors who burn and loot. The demonstrations are peppered with hate speech, profanity, and guys with sagging pants that show their underwear.

Decency, dignity and decorum. On May 31, 2020, during the George Floyd protests in Boston, Massachusetts, a peaceful protest turned violent as Antifa and BLM activists went on a rampage, destroying at least 16 statues and memorials. The *mobocrats* sprayed graffiti on a statue of George Washington, a 9/11 memorial, a WWI memorial, a WWII memorial, an Armenian genocide memorial, anti-lynching memorials, the Freedman's Memorial featuring Abraham Lincoln, and the Soldiers and Sailors Monument atop a hill on Boston Common. The Soldiers and Sailors Monument was dedicated to the memory of Massachusetts soldiers and sailors who died in the American Civil War to end slavery.

The *mobocrats* even desecrated the memorial to Robert Gould Shaw and the Massachusetts 54th Regiment at the edge of the Boston Common. In the name of peace and justice, BLM *mobocrats* desecrated the memorial with graffiti, declaring, "No justice, no peace," Black Lives Matter," Police are pigs," and a number of vulgar words. The bizarre irony in this stupid act of violence and destruction of public property was that the memorial was dedicated to the black soldiers of the 54th Massachusetts Regiment and Colonel Shaw, who fought to end Democratic systemic slavery.

One brave member of the black 54th Regiment was William Carney. Carney was born a slave in Norfolk, Virginia. He escaped from Democrat slavery to freedom through the Underground Railroad and settled in the free state of Massachusetts. Carney joined the 54th in March of 1863 and took part in the July 18, 1863, Battle of Fort Wagner in Charleston, South Carolina. When the Yankee color guard was killed, Carney grabbed Old Glory. While being shot a number of times, he brought Old Glory through the battlefield to the Yankee lines. As he handed it to another black soldier of the 54th, he declared "Boys, I only did my duty; the old flag never touched the ground!"

For his bravery, William Carney received the Congressional Medal of Honor. He was a man of dignity, decorum, and courageous content of character. He longed for Martin Luther King's American Dream 100 years before his famous speech at the Lincoln Memorial, which BLM also attacked. What is behind the ugly lack of decency, dignity, and decorum, and the cowardly lawless character when BLM activists and Antifa *mobocrat* thugs show such disrespect to America's freedom fighters? That is the topic of our next chapter.

Chapter 4

Socialism, Symbolism, and Statues

"Tear down the racist statues and the racist capitalist system" was the Socialist Appeal headline on June 22, 2020. Socialist Appeal, which calls itself a "Marxist organization which stands for the socialist transformation of society," was elated that BLM and Antifa activists had desecrated and/or destroyed a number of statues throughout Great Britain, Europe, Australia, the United States, and other parts of the world. From destroying and desecrating statues of slaveholder Robert Milligan and slave trader Edward Colston to the PM of the UK Winston Churchill and many, many more, international BLM Marxists, Antifa, and leftists are hell bent on the socialist transformation of English, American, and world civilization.

Outside of the London, England, headquarters of the BBC, the Broadcasting House, there is a black marble statue of George Orwell. The inscription behind the statue is Orwell's words from an unused preface to his classic novel *Animal*

Farm. It reads, "If liberty means anything at all, it means the right to tell people what they do not want to hear."

In this era of violent leftist iconoclasm, Antifa and BLM *mobocrats* cry out, "This is what democracy looks like" while they destroy public and private property. Many times they aim for a variety of statues they deem sacrilegious in their cultic world of utopian madness and mob-rule. Their goal? Was the goal of Marxist revolutionary Che Guevara's *"hombre Nuevo"* (the "new man"), made in the image of Friedrich Nietzsche's *"Ubermensch"* (the "superman"), also the goal of a new godless society shaped by nihilistic insanity where all facts, logic, and moral values are meaningless.

These iconoclast *mobocrats* cannot be reasoned with as they have appointed themselves the high priests of their new pure religion of postmodern absolutes in which historical and empirical evidence is pointless. In their universe, historical knowledge is useless, and language is to be introverted and perverted, unless of course it's their "knowledge" and their "language" shaped by narratives of lies and half-truths. Like the anti-Semite Henry Ford, they declare, "History is more or less bunk. It is tradition. We don't want tradition. We want to live in the present and the only history that is worth a tinker's damn is the history we make today."

These iconoclast *mobocrats* want to not only erase the history they deem inappropriate, but they want to also make history as they transform America into their Marxist image. The erasure of history leads to the tyranny of the present. They do not want us to have the "liberty to tell them what they do not want to hear." They only want to take down, erase, destroy, and obliterate every symbol, statue, painting, book, song, movie, and person that they deem evil and that does not fit their new man and new society of utopian perfection. They want to shut you up if you dare challenge their atheistic apostolic bad news that America is irredeemably racist. This lefty iconoclastic *mobocratic* religion is the deification of arrogant man/anarchy man/ mob-rule man who knows not decency, dignity, decorum, and democracy.

These iconoclast *mobocrats* are not open to dialogue, discussion, and democratic debate; they are driven by madness to storm the barricades of "Western oppression" and mandate in their imaginary world of utopian purity that no man or woman shall ever violate their faultless façade or dare speak a contrary opinion.

In George Orwell's classic dystopian novel *1984*, he warns,

> Every record has been destroyed or falsified, every book rewritten, every picture has been repainted, every statue and street building has been renamed, every date has been altered. And the process is continuing day by day and minute by minute. History has stopped. Nothing exists except an endless present in which the Party is always right.

Even the great writer George Orwell is not safe from their destructive claws in their insane slippery slope to tyranny. Eric Blair (George Orwell) lived in Burma in the 1920s as an officer in the British Imperial Police Force. Wearing black boots and khaki jodhpurs, Orwell was a part of a racist police force that enforced British colonial rule over the colored indigenous population.

Attention Antifa, BLM activists, and iconoclast *mobocrats*: if you are to be consistent, it is time to tear down Orwell's London statue! His statute is done in black, and as you preach, that is cultural appropriation. When you're done with him, you can go for Dafoe, Dante, Darwin, Dickens, Dostoyevsky, and thousands more. Shall we list their "sins," those of you who are pure and perfect, where everything is impure in your bizarre self righteous dystopian world where history, facts and context mean nothing?

There has been a movement for a number of years now to take down the statues, memorials, and paintings of Confederate Civil War historical figures located primarily in the South. In recent years, a number of statues, memorials, and schools named after Robert E. Lee, Stonewall Jackson, John C. Calhoun, Jefferson Davis, Nathan Bedford Forrest, and many more Confederates have been taken down or renamed.

Anybody who knows me knows I am not a fan of the CSA—the Confederate States of America. I have written extensively on their rebellion against the United States of America and their desire to create the antithesis of liberty here on American soil. The CSA was a racist republic dedicated to the advancement and preservation of slavery.

Here is my point. Yes, it's true that most of the Confederate memorials and statues were put up by the Democratic United Daughters of the Confederacy. They were part of a Southern Democratic education effort to spread the myth that the Confederacy wasn't fighting for slavery but for "states' rights," and that the slavery they did have wasn't all that bad. In reality, these Dixie Daughters were not only trying to instill white pride into a defeated southern society, but they were also rewriting history in the name of Anglo-Saxon supremacy. This is the Democratic institutionalized racism we destroyed many years ago.

With that being said, I know that a few of my readers will not agree with me on either side of this issue, but if these Confederate memorials are to be taken down, it should be done through democratic means in which the citizens of the area involved pass legislation to remove them legally and properly. The memorials can then be placed into museums to teach our youth about the historical Democratic Party's institutionalized racism. To have iconoclastic *mobocrats* violate the law and illegally destroy public and/or private property is not liberal democracy—it is illiberal *mobocracy*. Additionally, and much more egregious, it feeds the passions of the mob to extend their self-righteous priggish iconoclasm throughout America and the world involving many other historical figures from presidents to philosophers.

For example, the absolutely beautiful 1511 *The School of Athens* by the Renaissance painter Raphael features at its center the famous "white" Greek philosophers Plato and Aristotle. In his book *Politics*, written in the 300s B.C., Aristotle writes that some people by nature are fit to be slaves: "For that some should rule and others be ruled is not only necessary, but expedient; from the hour of their birth, some are marked out for subjugation, others for rule. Slavery is both expedient and right." Plato's classic work *Republic* is full of illiberal remarks defending slavery.

Does that mean Raphael's *The School of Athens* is to be desecrated or destroyed? Or that all statues of Plato and Aristotle are to be destroyed? Where does this madness stop? Will they come after all the sins of Newton, Joan of Arc, Shakespeare, John Locke, Thomas Paine, Michelangelo, Augustine, Aquinas, Kant, Voltaire, Bertrand Russell, Edmund Burke, Arthur Schopenhauer, Karl Marx, Kierkegaard, Sartre, Camus, Foucault, Derrida, William James, Tolstoy, Hume, and thousands more?

In 2017, after a number of Confederate statues were desecrated and/or destroyed, President Trump and a number of people (including me) warned that these *mobocratic* actions were going to lead to similar actions against Presidents Washington, Jefferson, Madison, Jackson, etc. Comedians including Stephen Colbert and John Oliver and Democratic politicians such as Nancy Pelosi and Chuck Schumer ridiculed President Trump as a fool, a simpleton whose hyperbole on the statues wasn't fitting for a president.

President Trump was spot on, warning us about the slippery slope that would go way beyond Confederate statues and symbolism. In 2020, during the George Floyd riots, besides desecrating and destroying a number of Confederate memorials and statues, the iconoclastic *mobocrats* desecrated and destroyed statues of Presidents Washington, Jefferson, Madison, Jackson, Grant, and even the Great Emancipator, Abraham Lincoln. They even desecrated the Lincoln Memorial, which Martin Luther King loved and used as the backdrop to his wonderful August 1963 speech, "I Have a Dream."

On the eve of July 4, 2020, President Trump delivered a speech at the foot of Mount Rushmore National Memorial in South Dakota in which he defended American presidents and heroes and attacked what he called the "new far-left fascism." The lefty activist media declared it was "dystopian," "dark and divisive," "racist," and "fascist," and MSNBC's Chris Matthews called it "Hitlerian."

I believe it was a monumental speech. The president impassionedly declared,

> Today, we pay tribute to the exceptional lives and extraordinary legacies of George Washington, Thomas Jefferson, Abraham Lincoln, and Teddy Roosevelt. I am here as your president to proclaim before the country and before the world: This monument will never be desecrated, these heroes will never be defaced, their legacy will never, ever be destroyed, their achievements will never be forgotten, and Mount Rushmore will stand forever as an eternal tribute to our forefathers and to our freedom.

> We gather tonight to herald the most important day in the history of nations: July 4th, 1776. At those words, every American heart should swell with pride. Every American family should cheer with delight. And every American patriot should be filled with joy, because each of you lives in the most magnificent country in the history of the world....

> Our Founders launched not only a revolution in government, but a revolution in the pursuit of justice, equality, liberty, and prosperity. No nation

has done more to advance the human condition than the United States of America. And no people have done more to promote human progress than the citizens of our great nation....

Our Founders boldly declared that we are all endowed with the same divine rights given to us by our Creator in Heaven. And that which God has given us, we will allow no one, ever, to take away—ever.

Seventeen seventy-six represented the culmination of thousands of years of western civilization and the triumph not only of spirit, but of wisdom, philosophy, and reason.

And yet, as we meet here tonight, there is a growing danger that threatens every blessing our ancestors fought so hard for, struggles, they bled to secure. Our nation is witnessing a merciless campaign to wipe out our history, defame our heroes, erase our values, and indoctrinate our children.

Angry mobs are trying to tear down statues of our Founders, deface our most sacred memorials, and unleash a wave of violent crime in our cities. Many of these people have no idea why they are doing this, but some know exactly what they are doing....

In our schools, our newsrooms, even our corporate boardrooms, there is a new far left fascism that demands absolute allegiance. If you do not speak its language, perform its rituals, recite its mantras, and follow its commandments, then you will be censored, banished, blacklisted, persecuted, and punished....

Make no mistake: this left-wing cultural revolution is designed to overthrow the American Revolution.... To make this possible, they are determined to tear down every statue, symbol, and memory of our national heritage....

We want free and open debate, not speech codes and cancel culture. We embrace tolerance, not prejudice.

The *mobocrats* do not want free and open debate. They are at war with life, liberty, and decency in America. They are profoundly intolerant and fascist in their words and actions, and they are hell bent on destroying our heavenly heritage with their Marxist cultural revolution to eliminate our republic under God.

In Madison, Wisconsin, at the University of Wisconsin in front of Bascom Hall, there is a beautiful statue of President Lincoln. Every time I give speeches on campus, I try to visit Lincoln's statue for inspiration. Two lefty student organizations, the Black Student Union and Student Inclusion Coalition, along with BLM activists, are demanding that it be taken down. Black Student Union President Nalah McWhorter said, "For him to be at the top of Bascom [Hill] as a powerful placement on our campus, it's a single-handed symbol of white supremacy. Just because he was anti-slavery doesn't mean he was pro-black." The Student Inclusion Coalition, whose logo is browns and blacks declaring, "We expect, we demand," and whose byline is "Advocates for the social, academic, and emotional wellness of all marginalized students at the University of Wisconsin-Madison," put out a flyer that listed all the anti-black and anti-native sins of Abraham Lincoln, insisting that his statue be taken down.

There is something much more sinister than Lincoln's sins behind BLM and lefty calls to destroy Lincoln's statue and legacy. This is the world of "identity *mobocracy*," where lefty *mobocrats* have created a war of proletariat blacks versus bourgeois whites, LGBTQ versus the "Western prescribed nuclear family" and the cisgender white male. BLM and their comrades are creating a vicious, violent, divisive tribal warfare versus our beautiful First Amendment and our constitutional republic under God.

On June 22, 2020, Devonere Johnson, a BLM activist who goes by YeShua Musa, walked into Cooper's Tavern in the heart of downtown Madison, Wisconsin. While blasting music from a boom box, he demanded to the owner: "Give me money or I will break windows! Venmo me the money! You are all KKK!"

The next day, June 23, 2020, at approximately 12:35 PM, Johnson returned to Cooper's Tavern with a megaphone and a baseball bat with the words, "Black lives matter" painted on it, started yelling and calling the white patrons racists, "I am F****ing disturbing the F***k out of this restaurant and I got a F****ing bat." Johnson demanded money again and free food, otherwise he and hundreds of protestors would burn down the tavern.

The owner called the Madison police. They detained Johnson, but he tried to escape twice. On June 26, 2020, federal authorities charged Johnson with extortion saying, "The citizens of the city and state need to know that they are protected in their businesses, their homes, and the community. And that starts with upholding and enforcing the law. Extortion is not activism. It is a crime and will not be tolerated."

However, once the word got out that a fellow BLM comrade was arrested on June 23, 2020, following Johnson's arrest, BLM activists spread the word and called for a protest in front of the Madison jail, yelling out, "F**k 12" (a reference to narcotics police), and "Black Lives Matter!" Black Lives Matter activist Ebony Sarton cried to the *Madison Times* reporter saying, "I'm emotionally hurt because never in my life would I have thought that someone who trusted me with their life enough to come save them would be going through this. Yeshua is my friend and I think he is being targeted, and it's not fair."

Emotions and feelings were feeding the iconoclastic *mobocrats* as they proceeded to Madison's Capitol at the end of State Street and they began smashing windows and lights at the State House. They attacked Democratic State Senator Tim Carpenter for taking pictures of the riots. Two statues, one of Wisconsin's "Forward" motto and the other of abolitionist Colonel Hans Christian Heg, were destroyed. Yes, you read that right. Colonel Heg was an abolitionist who fought in the U.S. Union Army to end slavery. The iconoclastic *mobocrats* ripped the statue off its pedestal, ripped off the head, and threw it into the nearby Lake Monona. The words "Black is beautiful" was spray painted above Hans Christian Heg's name on the plinth that held Heg's statue.

Rena Yehuda Newman recently graduated from University of Wisconsin-Madison. In the 1960s, the University of Wisconsin became known as the Midwest bastion of New Left intellectuals, many of whom were influenced by Frankfurt School Marxists. UW-Madison is known as the "Midwest UC-Berkeley." It still is to this day. I love Madison, Wisconsin—it is a beautiful city with its campus situated between two lovely Wisconsin lakes. I go to Madison often as I have been involved in speaking at various historical/ political conferences and on occasion to UW students at YAF (Young Americans for Freedom) events.

Back to Rena Yehuda Newman. Newman is transgender and uses the pronouns "they/them," identifies as non-binary, and feels "they" don't fit into the binary groups of male and female, he/she. I don't know if Newman is a he/she or a she/ he. Oy vey! This "gender-binary" male Baby Boomer already screwed up by trying to identify "them." I'm so verklempt! Do English and biology mean anything anymore?

Newman was a history major and served as the student historian in residence at the University of Wisconsin Archives. Newman is a hard-core white leftist BLM activist and editor-in-chief for the left-wing *New Voice Magazine*. Newman responded to the Devonere Johnson riots with an article titled, "Don't Mourn for Statues; imagine what can flourish in their place." I quote "they/them" extensively to illustrate the absolute madness of the iconoclastic *mobocrats* and the world they live in.

In the article, Newman ignores the criminal behavior of Johnson or Musa and blames the Madison police for the "violent arrest of Yeshua Musa for using a megaphone in public." Newman says BLM organized the demonstration because of the arrest of Musa. They demanded that no pictures or videos be taken so police could not use them to arrest the protestors. Newman downplays the violent attack on Democrat State Senator Tim Carpenter, who displeased the BLM protestors because he was taking pictures. Newman then goes on to attack "white liberal progressive Democrats" for being angry over the toppling of non-Confederate statues.

Newman writes, "In the morning, as Wisconsin residents awoke to the news of the toppled statues, I noticed an outrage begin to form. Frighteningly, I found this outrage fomenting through the Facebook statuses and think pieces published by people who talk of equality, who proudly vote Democrat, who may even have yard signs that say, 'Black Lives Matter.'"

Newman then goes on to say,

> Compared to a monument of Robert E. Lee, and for many Democratic voters of Wisconsin and America more broadly, these downed statues seem like symbols of a liberal America, a progressive America. The unfortunate reality is that these people were angrier about toppled statues than stolen Black lives—and that these angry people are white like me. Once examined more deeply, these statues and the white desire to defend them reveals a deeper truth about American racism which implicates more of us than just those flying the Confederate flag.

Newman is now showing us the "deeper truth" behind his/her "white leftism" and her/his "white-mob-rule" worldview and mindset. This white Zoomer American has a disdain not only for conservative Christian Boomers like me, but also for the white liberal and progressive Democrats with BLM signs in their yards. First, Newman tells us how "white" the toppled Forward statue was, as it was sculpted by a white woman as a symbol of white manifest destiny in America. According to Newman, this "white lady liberty" symbolizes the "Forward" move of the federal government massacring the Ojibwe Nation and being forced out of Wisconsin territory.

Newman concludes about the white racist Wisconsin Forward statue by stating,

> This statue's history cannot be disentangled from the monument itself. White Americans' defense of such a statue is in fact a defense of something much darker—a desire to believe an American mythology that does not contain the capacity to acknowledge the violent histories of racism, exploitation and Native genocide entangled in the white liberals' most precious symbols.

To Newman, racism and genocide are entangled in the white liberals' most precious symbols. Newman's "wokeness" eviscerates white liberals, but Newman's not done. Next is the "mythology of the Civil War," in which Newman goes after abolitionist Colonel Hans Christian Heg.

Newman states,

The second downed statue was that of Hans Christian Heg, paraded as a "Civil War hero" by local news outlets.... Heg was both an abolitionist and a settler-colonist, involved in the famous "Gold Rush" that displaced and later caused the murder of indigenous people in California. If one wishes to defend Heg, one must reckon with his full complexity. If one wishes to celebrate the American abolition of slavery, one must also reckon with a Civil War history that does not exonerate the Union of its deep racism. What better example of this than white Wisconsinites preferring to commemorate abolition by celebrating white abolitionists like Heg instead of black historical figures? Given Heg's abolitionist views, many critics of the protest have seen his statue's removal as senseless. But when we look to the world that we truly wish to build and the figures we truly wish to commemorate, I am certain that we can do better than a statue of Heg. And besides, I feel quite certain that a true Abolitionist would appreciate the removal of a white statue for the sake of black liberation.

In Newman's "woke" world, her liberators and her statues must be "true Abolitionists" with a pristine pedigree of perfection not tainted by the white world of colonialism and white supremacy. Newman writes,

Given the history and symbolism embedded in these statues, it is grotesque that their removal has evoked more ire from white liberals than the actual murder of black people; including murders that are close to home.... The action that took place last week at the Wisconsin Capitol removed two statues whose symbology is not of the explicitly racist, slave-owning Confederacy, but represents another dangerous and insidious America in denial of its taste for white supremacy. It is unwise to worship idols of an America that insulate the white public from facing the legacy of slavery in police brutality and settler colonialism.... It is easy to deride statues of the racist Confederacy, but especially in a place like Madison, it is more meaningful, to topple symbols of white liberal hypocrisy. Liberal white people must avoid the trap of being Martin Luther King's "White moderate."

To Newman, even white progressive Madison liberals with BLM signs in their yards have an insidious taste for white supremacy, and it is the duty, the righteous calling of the "woke" white folk in BLM and other liberating organizations to destroy "the symbols of white liberal hypocrisy! This moment in the American present demands a more holistic, complex, and frankly, more painful reckoning with American history."

Newman would probably agree with the hashtag #CancelHamilton, with which thousands of lefties demand that the very popular and successful Broadway play *Hamilton* be cancelled because "the Founding Father's work in the slave trade is completely glossed over in Lin-Manuel Miranda's musical." The man behind the call to cancel *Hamilton* is Marxist black activist Ajamu Baraka who, like Newman, attacks white progressive liberals or even Barack Obama, whom he called "an Uncle Tom president."

Baraka and Newman would probably love the fact that the Hispanic playwright Lin-Manuel Miranda cast *Hamilton* with black, Hispanic, and Asian-American actors as the Founding Fathers and other dead white people in history. White actors were not welcome. But Baraka and other hardcore *mobocrats* cannot tolerate *Hamilton* because "The play and now movie Hamilton is racist buffoonery and revisionist history meant to make liberal white folks feel good about their collaboration with the colonial project [known] as the U.S. and its racist imperialist project abroad." One Twitter response was "Hamilton was a slave trader. Tear down the statues NOW and #CancelHamilton!"

Baraka and Newman and their iconoclastic *mobocratic* ilk are classic examples of the quintessential woke Zoomers. They consider themselves enlightened with so much "wokeness" that they become the high priests and priestesses of the cleansing of the present-day American society. They also believe the white supremacist past must be eliminated in totality from our history and culture. Newman and leftists, through mob-rule, want to build a utopian world of perfection where all past sins have been scrubbed clean from our so-called white supremacy society, a world where perfection in humanity is the daily duty of the lefty "Cultural Thought Police."

One wonders what Newman, Black Lives Matter, Antifa, and all the *mobocrats* would do with America's Statue of Liberty. In 1886, the Statue of Liberty was a symbol of liberal democratic republican government and a celebration of the USA's victory over the CSA and the abolition of slavery.

The creator of Lady Liberty was the French political thinker, U.S. Constitution expert, and abolitionist Edouard de Laboulaye. He was an admirer of President Lincoln and the co-founder of the French Anti-Slavery Society, which called on all nations to abolish slavery. Laboulaye's statue of *Liberty Enlightening the World* not only represented liberal democratic republicanism around the world but also America's 1776 birth of freedom, dedicated to the end of oppression and servitude. A broken shackle and chain lie at Lady Liberty's right foot, disappearing beneath her skirt and reappearing in front of her left foot. The broken shackle and chain beautifully symbolize the abolition of slavery in America.

Fortunately for America and her black citizens, the institutionalized Democratic Jim Crow that plagued the South and other parts of the rest of America was destroyed through the valiant efforts of multicolored civil rights activists. Those activists helped shape civil rights legislation of the 1960s, thus fulfilling the dream of Laboulaye's statue for millions of people from around the world. They still flock to our shores to experience the prosperity, liberty, and social mobility of the United States of America, the greatest republic in the history of the world.

Unfortunately, on July 4, 2020, a statue of Frederick Douglass was torn down in Rochester, New York, on the 168th anniversary of one of Douglass' most famous speeches. Douglass and his speech will be a key part of the following chapter.

Chapter 5

Frederick Douglass' "4th of July" Speech and Zinn's Sins

I'm writing this on the 4th of July, 2020. This morning as I scanned social media, I noticed a number of people, many of whom were BLM supporters, had put out a short NPR (National Public Radio) video titled *Frederick Douglass' Descendants Deliver His 'Fourth of July' Speech*. In fact, many of the people who were posting this NPR video were high-school and middle-school social studies teachers. In fact, one teacher said, "Worth 7 mins of your time on the 4th of July weekend!" Another said, "This is as relevant today as it was 170 years ago." So I watched it.

There were five very bright high-school and middle-school black descendants of Frederick Douglass who said that they were the "great, great, great grandchildren" of Frederick Douglass. In a very poised manner, they each delivered a short part of the famous Douglass "4th of July" speech, which lasted about four minutes. They all shared a few sentences from their great, great, great grandfather's famous 1852 speech.

As I heard their quite truncated version of the speech, it reminded me of a similar version of the famous Frederick Douglass "4th of July" speech done in 2004 with James Earl Jones as the narrator. I did a little digging, and sure enough, I was correct. The 2020 4th of July NPR speech was not a brand new "truncated" version of the Douglass speech, but it was pretty much the same James Earl Jones rendition 16 years later with younger readers. The 2004 version was sponsored by the Vermont Humanities Council and introduced by the Marxist historian Howard Zinn. Both the NPR 2020 version and the 2004 James Earl Jones version lasted about four minutes.

The original 1852 Frederick Douglass "4th of July" speech was about one hour and six minutes. So the truncated 4th of July speeches were missing about one hour and two minutes, or approximately 94% of the speech. The reason I knew this is because I have used Frederick Douglass' great speech for many years during my "Slavery–Civil War" unit at the high schools and the university where I have taught. I have read the speech a number of times before, and as a student of Frederick Douglass, I knew that there were some very important details, ideas, words, and facts that the "6% speech" left out. Here is the script from the four-minute 2004 James Earl Jones version of the Frederick Douglass speech introduced by the Marxist historian Howard Zinn. As you read it, notice the negative aspects of America that Douglass is rightfully speaking of. I will address that later:

Frederick Douglass [read by James Earl Jones]:
Fellow citizens, pardon me, allow me to ask, why
am I called upon to speak here today? What have
I, or those I represent, to do with your national
independence? Are the great principles of political
freedom and of natural justice, embodied in that
Declaration of Independence, extended to us? And
am I, therefore, called upon to bring our humble
offering to the national altar, and to confess the
benefits and express devout gratitude for the
blessings resulting from your independence to us?

I am not included within the pale of this glorious
anniversary! Your high independence only reveals
the immeasurable distance between us. The
blessings in which you this day rejoice are not
enjoyed in common. The rich inheritance of justice,
liberty, prosperity, and independence bequeathed
by your fathers is shared by you, not by me. The
sunlight that brought life and healing to you has
brought stripes and death to me. This Fourth of
July is yours, not mine. You may rejoice, I must
mourn. To drag a man in fetters into the grand
illuminated temple of liberty, and call upon him
to join you in joyous anthems, were inhuman
mockery and sacrilegious irony. Do you mean,
citizens, to mock me, by asking me to speak today?

What, to the American slave, is your Fourth of
July? I answer: a day that reveals to him, more
than all other days of the year, the gross injustice
and cruelty to which he is a constant victim. To
him, your celebration is a sham; your boasted

liberty, an unholy license; your national greatness, swelling vanity; your sounds of rejoicing are empty and heartless; your denunciation of tyrants, brass fronted impudence; your shouts of liberty and equality, hollow mockery; your prayers and hymns, your sermons and thanksgivings, with all your religious parade and solemnity, are, to Him, mere bombast, fraud, deception, impiety, and hypocrisy—a thin veil to cover up crimes that would disgrace a nation of savages. There is not a nation of the earth guilty of practices more shocking and bloody than are the people of these United States at this very hour.

At a time like this, scorching irony, not convincing argument, is needed. O! had I the ability, and could reach the nation's ear, I would, today, pour forth a stream, a fiery stream of biting ridicule, blasting reproach, withering sarcasm, and stern rebuke. For it is not light that is needed, but fire; it is not the gentle shower, but thunder. We need the storm, the whirlwind, the earthquake. The feeling of the nation must be quickened; the conscience of the nation must be roused; the propriety of the nation must be startled; the hypocrisy of the nation must be exposed; and the crimes against God and man must be proclaimed and denounced.

The NPR 2020 version is pretty much the same words but with sentences moved around. At the end of the July 2020 version, the five teenage descendants of Douglass said that their great, great, great grandfather's words were "relevant with today's protests" [BLM George Floyd protests], that

"people are oppressed," and "I think in many ways we are
still slaves to the notion that it will never get better." Similar
words were said by Howard Zinn and the people on the 4th
of July panel at Vermont Humanities Council in 2004 after
doing their truncated version of Douglass' "4th of July"
speech.

So what is going on here? Did you notice the righteous angry
rhetoric by Douglass? Did you notice the passionate attack
on the continued practice of slavery in America? Those four
minutes in his speech are speaking an ugly truth about
America in 1852, an ugly truth that needs to be learned
to fully appreciate the horrible nature and conditions
of slavery. I use Douglass' speech to help my students
understand the bloody struggle for freedom experienced
by black slaves and white abolitionists. I also reveal the
hypocrisy of those who proclaim those wonderful 1776
words "all men are created equal" and yet allow inequality
and bondage to flourish across the land. Douglass' words
were needed to be heard in 1852, and they are needed to be
heard today, but in *full context* with the telling of the *full
American story* in all its infamy and glory.

To understand the modern-day academic emphasis on the
infamous parts of American history, it helps to know who
Howard Zinn is. The English rock 'n' roll band The Who in
their 1969 song "Pinball Wizard" sang, "Ever since I was
a young boy, I've played the silver ball; from Soho down
to Brighton, I must have played them all." Well, I've been
from Soho down to Brighton, England, when I attended
the University of Brighton in 1980, studying American
and European history. I was introduced by a very left-wing
professor to an American history textbook titled *A People's*

History of the United States by Howard Zinn, a self-proclaimed communist professor at Boston University.

Zinn considered himself a Marxist social justice warrior who used his teaching platform, books, and plays as a tool to influence his students into transforming the United States of America into a socialist nation. *A People's History* has been assigned as reading in many middle schools, high schools, and colleges across the United States and has sold over two million copies since 1980. The problem with Zinn's very popular work is that it has a very twisted history that is viciously anti-capitalistic, anti-Christian, and anti-conservative, written to fit his Marxist aims.

In Howard Zinn's Marxist academic world, America's Founders are all about the "capitalistic" pursuit of exploitation and profit at the expense of the people, especially white people exploiting and oppressing all other people groups, especially black slaves. According to Zinn, by feigning a democratic rhetoric of life, liberty, equality, and the pursuit of happiness, white Americans have been lying to the American people since its beginning.

July 4, 1776, to Zinn is not one of the great seminal events in world history reflecting the exceptional nature of the United States, but it is when oppressive totalitarian tragedies have been perpetuated by white bourgeois supremacy. In classic Marxian language, Zinn says of his goal as a writer and teacher of history:

> I wanted my writing of history and my teaching of history to be a part of a social struggle.... I wanted to be a part of history and not just a recorder and teacher of history. So that kind of attitude towards

history, history itself as a political act, has always informed my writing and my teaching.

Zinn's books have indoctrinated millions of American youth with his anti-American Marxian worldview.

The United States is not a perfect nation. No nation is. I have been teaching the "good, the bad, and the ugly" about American history for well over 30 years. However, with that being said, the United States of America is still an exceptional nation whose good has brought life, liberty, equality, and justice for millions and millions here and across the world. Unfortunately, Comrade Zinn focuses only on the *sin*—the bad and the ugly—in America as he attacks our Founders as white money-grubbing charlatans. He also calls their traditional Christian values "bourgeois" claptrap. Zinn is so "in" in our culture and our colleges that his friend, Hollywood actor Matt Damon in the movie *Goodwill Hunting*, recommended that people should read Zinn's *A People's History*.

Do you remember the line from The Who—"From Soho down to Brighton"? Soho is an area in the west end of London, England, and it is where, in the Red Lion pub, that Karl Marx wrote much of his evil book *The Communist Manifesto*. Howard Zinn, an admirer of *The Communist Manifesto* and its author, wrote a play called *Marx in Soho*. Zinn's play depicts a resurrected Marx who now lives in Soho, New York City, and defends his Communist ideas versus the 100 million–plus killed in his name. *Marx in Soho* is a clarion defense of the principles of Marxism and the "wonderful" ideas of Karl Marx's scientific socialism where capitalism will be destroyed along with any nation that practices such "evil" free enterprise activities.

Zinn's books, plays, and teachings are primarily a diatribe against the United States of America and a defense of the evil ideas of Marxism. Zinn's works are so popular in high schools and colleges that there is a Zinn Education Project. The project provides lesson plans, curricula, conferences, and seminars where ten of thousands of teachers are indoctrinated with Zinn's sins against our republic under God. Zinn hated that God and taught against Him throughout his career. While Howard Zinn died in 2010, his ideas live on in his books, plays, and disciples, many of whom are U.S. history teachers in our middle schools, high schools, and colleges today.

So what does Zinn's influence on our educational system have to do with Frederick Douglass and America's birthday in 1776? Everything. The philosophy of the schoolroom in one generation will be the philosophy of government and many citizens in the next.

We see lies about America being disseminated daily in our classrooms as teachers act as social justice warriors and bombard our kids with half truths and deconstructed cultural Marxist versions of American history. These perversions of our history are indoctrinating our youth with a profound anti-1776, anti-American, Marxist worldview that now takes it to the streets, desecrating and destroying historical symbols while demanding politically correct lefty group-think and speech. If you challenge their bogus truncated history, you are attacked as a racist, fascist, Nazi, and all the other sundry derisive invectives the left loves to use in their arsenal of Orwellian gobbledygook.

National Public Radio is not the only educational entity putting out truncated versions of Frederick Douglass' 4th of July speech. For many years now, there have been many different groups and individuals, in some form or fashion, cherry picking sentences from Douglass' speech and disseminating them throughout social media on every 4th of July. One such individual was former secretary of labor under President Clinton, Democrat Robert Reich.

As an unabashed lefty-progressive, Robert Reich is an admirer of Marxist Howard Zinn, and he uses his materials when he speaks and teaches at UC-Berkeley. On July 3, 2020, Reich posted on Twitter the four-minute NPR Douglass 4th of July speech. On his Facebook page, he posted a meme with a picture of Frederick Douglass. Reich introduced the meme with these words: "From Frederick Douglass' speech 'What to the Slave is the Fourth of July?' on July 5th, 1852." Here's the quote Reich chose: "The rich inheritance of justice, liberty, prosperity, and independence bequeathed by your fathers is shared by you, not by me. This Fourth of July is yours, not mine. The sunlight that brought life and healing to you brought stripes and death to me. You may rejoice; I must mourn."

Robert Reich very selectively pulls out of context the negative, the bad, and the ugly aspects of Douglass' speech without mentioning the good and positive parts of the speech that would affirm the greatness of America. Reich, like many in the Democratic Party and lefty academia, are determined to construct and teach a narrative of America today that is an evil white supremacist nation permeated with institutionalized racism. Robert Reich, as a Rhodes scholar, a graduate of Yale, and a professor at Harvard and UC-Berkeley, should know better than to violate the golden rule of using full context to properly understand language and the intention of the author. Reich, like many in academia and the activist media, twist history all the time to create an imbalanced false story of America.

Another example of deconstructing and twisting American history is ex-NFL football player Colin Kaepernick. On July 4, 2019, he quoted from Douglass' 4th of July speech, tweeting, "What have I, or those I represent, to do with your national independence? This Fourth of July is yours, not mine.... There is not a nation on the earth guilty of practices more shocking and bloody than are the people of these United States at this very hour."

Kaepernick, like Robert Reich, cherry picks out only those negative and bad parts that paint an America in the most demeaning light, perpetually ruled by white supremacy. Kaepernick ignores the full context of what Douglass' full ideas and goals were in delivering his 1852 speech. At the end of his great speech, Douglass declared, "I, therefore, leave off where I began, with hope. While drawing encouragement from the 'Declaration of Independence,' the great principles it contains, and the genius of American institutions, my spirit is also cheered by the obvious tendencies of the age."

Kaepernick repeated his anti-American diatribes again on July 4, 2020, when he tweeted, "black ppl have been dehumanized, brutalized, criminalized + terrorized by America for centuries, & are expected to join your commemoration of 'independence,' while you enslaved our ancestors. We reject your celebration of white supremacy and look forward to liberation for all."

Where did Colin Kaepernick develop and learn his anti-4th of July worldview? He learned from Howard Zinn's works, of course, from many other Marxist academics when he attended the University of California-Berkeley, and while playing for the San Francisco 49ers as quarterback. Kaepernick's refusal to participate in our National Anthem during NFL games in 2016 had a big influence on many of our youth. He also influenced many in the world of academics, including my colleagues who, like him, posted on social media the four-minute NPR Douglass 4th of July speech. Here is my problem with using only the four-minute "6%" Douglass speech.

I use this four-minute version to teach not only Douglass' amazing oratory and mind, but also about the horrible world of slavery and the hypocrisy that went along with it. I have always taught my students the good, the bad, and the ugly in American history and that *context is key*. I put on the board the very first day of school, "Context is King!" to help my students understand the proper use of language and history in full context. My students need to be aware of how people can take things out of context to create a false text and narrative that drives a pretext of half truths and misleading narratives.

Besides the context, I teach my students to "learn to discern" and "trust but verify." So I play the four-minute version and then we read and/or watch the actual whole one-hour and six-minute 4th of July speech by Frederick Douglass. Then we analyze it and discuss it for a wonderful lesson plan on not only a great American but also on how important it is to study primary historical documents in their *full context*. We also study how a possibly truncated or cherry-picked version of a document can distort and pervert the actual meanings and intent of the author and then used for a political and/or alternative agenda not intended by the author.

When analyzing Douglass' great speech, we see his brilliant thinking processes and his command of Christian-biblical literature and use of the Passover-Exodus theme of the Jewish people fighting to be free from the slavery and bondage in Egypt. We discuss the very clever structure of the speech and how it was given in the midst of many turbulent contexts: the Democratic Fugitive Slave Act, *Uncle Tom's Cabin*, Northern states dealing with Southern Democrats being upset with their state laws making blacks free, etc.

Douglass had three main parts of the speech. First, he addressed the audience as "fellow citizens" a number of times and then honored the genius of the Founding Fathers. He stated,

> Fellow citizens, I am not wanting in respect for the fathers of this republic. The signers of the Declaration of Independence were brave men. They were great men too.... They were statesmen, patriots, and heroes, and for the good they did, and the principles they contended for, I will unite with you to honor their memory.

It is why I, like Frederick Douglass, honor the memory of our Founders when I teach the American Revolution, but I also point out, like Douglass, some of their bad and ugly practices such as their defense of slavery, especially by the Southern Founders.

In part two of Douglass' speech, he boldly sounded like a Hebrew prophet, declaring that while the 1776 Declaration of Independence is a wonderful declaration of liberty and equality for all, "This Fourth of July is yours, not mine! The rich inheritance of justice, liberty, prosperity, and independence bequeathed by your fathers is shared by you, not by me. The sunlight that brought life and healing to you brought stripes and death to me." Sadly, Douglass was pointing out the hypocrisy that still existed in America in 1852, and he was trying to stir into the hearts and minds of his abolitionist audience that it was time to align the words of our great Declaration with great actions to abolish slavery. Most of the NPR/James Earl Jones four-minute versions of the speech were taken from part two of Douglass' speech.

In part three, we see that Douglass got the "Garrison Abolitionists" upset. The Garrison Abolitionists were followers of the famous William Lloyd Garrison, who taught that the U.S. Constitution was an evil pro-slavery document as Douglass did in his early years. However, after years of studying our constitutional republic, Douglass changed his thinking about our Constitution and embraced it passionately, declaring that our republic's Constitution was "a GLORIOUS LIBERTY DOCUMENT [caps his] full of principles and purposes, entirely hostile to the existence of slavery."

Once my students hear or read Douglass' full speech, they are amazed by what they learn about Douglass' love of our Founders, our 1776 Declaration of Independence, and our federal constitutional republic. They also begin to understand Lincoln's legal mind better and why he connected the Emancipation Proclamation to our 1776 Declaration of Independence. Plus, they learn why Martin Luther King Jr. used the words of both Douglass and Lincoln as he spoke his wonderful 1963 "I Have a Dream" speech in front of the Lincoln Memorial about the "magnificent words of the Constitution and the Declaration of Independence."

I hope and pray my colleagues and all of America will begin to do the same with Douglass' full speech.

Why is there so much disinformation and misinformation out there when it comes to American history? We've already covered the influence of the Marxist Frankfurt School and Marxist professors, including Howard Zinn's profound influence in America's schools through his books and the Zinn Education Project. But there is another fresh, new project out there, which has the goal of advancing Zinn's anti-American "bad and ugly" U.S. history with even more vehement determination than ever before. It is called the "1619 Project." This is the topic of our next chapter.

Chapter 6

1619 Project versus July 4, 1776

> Who controls the past, controls the future: who
> controls the present controls the past ... the past
> is whatever the records and the memories agree
> upon. And since the Party is in full control of all
> records, and in equally full control of the minds of
> its members, it follows that the past is whatever the
> Party chooses to make it.

In 1949, George Orwell wrote these words in his classic
work *1984* about rewriting and perverting history by a
controlling political party so the people are manipulated
by the lies of the past to control the present and the future.
Such is the case with the Democratic Party's endorsement
and utilization of the 1619 Project.

Orwell wrote those prophetic words 70 years before the
release of the *New York Times'* 1619 Project on August
19, 2019, with a 100-page edition in its Sunday magazine.
In the past year, the *New York Times* has spent over

$65 million on advertising its pseudo-American history propaganda project. On Facebook, with big 1619 numbers, they wrote, "The *New York Times* is launching the #1619Project, a collection of essays, criticism, and art about how the America we know today didn't start in 1776—it started in August 1619 when a ship carrying Africans landed in Virginia."

In another ad on Twitter, the *New York Times*, with a picture of black slaves in a cotton field and the caption "American Capitalism is Brutal. You Can Trace That to the Plantation," they declare:

> "In order to understand the brutality of American capitalism, you have to start on the plantation," writes Matthew Desmond for the #1619Project. "Given the choice between modernity and barbarism, prosperity and poverty, lawfulness and cruelty, democracy and totalitarianism, America chose all the above."

The Pulitzer Center reports that in less than a year, the 1619 Project is in more than 4,500 classrooms. Forty-five hundred classrooms and counting! The Black Lives Matter at School curriculum is also exploding in our schools across America. On July 8, 2020, *The Federalist* declared, "Black Lives Matter in Public Schools Is Turning Our Kids into Little Marxists." And we wonder why, between the Marxist Zinn Education Project, Black Lives Matter at School, and the 1619 Project, our youth are in our streets protesting, rioting, desecrating, and calling for the destruction of "white capitalism" and the dismantling of America's "white system of oppression." We know why.

The *mobocrats* have won the textbooks! They have won the curriculum, the classrooms, and the culture! The father of the Marxist Russian Revolution, Vladimir Lenin, loved to say, "Give me four years to teach the children and the seed I have sown will never be uprooted ... give us the child for eight years and it will be a Bolshevik forever!"

The legacy of the radical Marxist teachers of the 1960s, 70s, 80s, and 90s is their lasting indoctrination of far too many Generation Xers and Millennials. They have fallen in love with socialism and have learned to hate capitalism and whiteness while they ignore the extraordinary history of the United States. These Xers and Millennials are now not only teaching our Zoomers but are also teaching the future teachers of America and are in the HR departments of many of our corporations calling for the lefty Culture Thought Police.

This Boomer U.S. history teacher, a passionate lover of America, weeps when I see so many Zoomers falling for the lies of Zinn and the 1619 Project. They are joining in with the Antifa, BLM, leftist *mobocrats* in the classrooms and in the streets, and they are crying out, "This is what democracy looks like" as they deny free speech; desecrate, destroy, and violate private and public property; and attack many innocent people. This illiberal mob-rule is not what democracy looks like; this *mobocracy* is eroding the liberty foundation of this nation, opening the doors of oppression, control, and tyranny right before our eyes.

Nikole Hannah Jones, who loves to declare that "anti-black racism runs in the very DNA of this country," is the creator of the pseudo-historical 1619 Project. She will be partnering with Oprah Winfrey and Lionsgate to bring their imbalanced anti-American diatribe to TV and film. They have won the culture, and I guarantee they will bring this 1619 Project film into the classrooms of America. How strange for the anti-capitalist 1619 Project creator, millionaire Nikole Hannah Jones, to be working with billionaire Oprah, America's richest black American female, telling a story of our "evil white capitalistic nation."

Such oppression, such hypocrisy and purveyance of truncated and twisted history.

Jones, who calls herself "The Beyoncé of Journalism," on her Twitter account with a black backdrop picture of the date July 4, 1776, crossed out in white, and the date August 20, 1619, highlighted below it, wrote the *New York Times* debut essay for the 1619 Project. Her essay was a BLM hit but a historical disaster. It was attacked by dozens and dozens of American history professors, instructors, and teachers (including me) for its false premises and inaccurate presentation of U.S. history.

James McPhearson, James Oakes, Victoria Bynum, Sean Wilentz, and Gordon Woods, considered some of America's leading experts on early American history, responded to the 1619 Project in a letter sent to the *New York Times*, calling it "a very unbalanced, one-sided account ... wrong in so many ways ... not only ahistorical but actually anti-historical ... full of falsehoods and distortions."

These brilliant and renowned historians went on to say,

> These errors, which concern major events, cannot be described as interpretation or "framing";

they are matters of verifiable fact, which are the foundation of both honest scholarship and honest journalism. They suggest a displacement of historical understanding by ideology. Dismissal of objections on racial grounds—that they are the objections on racial grounds—that they are the objections of only "white historians"—has affirmed that displacement.

It is important to note that the aforementioned historians are all on the left side of the political spectrum. When they challenged the 1619 "historical narrative," they were accused of bias because they were white and blinded by their privilege. This sounds like a typical BLM *mobocrat* retort, doesn't it? Unfortunately for the 1619 Project, they can't use the "white" excuse when confronted by the black scholars of the 1776 Project, which was created to correct the historical inaccuracies and ideological disdain for America, free enterprise, and the exceptional nature of the American fight for freedom.

Black American historians, academics, and entrepreneurs such as Shelby Steele, Carol M. Swain, Jason D. Hill, John McWorther, Glenn Lowry, Clarence Page, Wilfred Riley, John Wood Jr., Ian Rowe, Coleman Cruz Hughes, Bob Woodson, and many, many more, challenge the major mistakes, imbalanced history, and over-stressed false premises of the 1619 Project. Guess what these 1776 Project academics and advocates are called? Yup, you got it right: "Uncle Toms" and "Aunt Jemimas." Where have we heard that before?

And to think that Nikole Hannah Jones, "The Beyoncé of Journalism," won a Pulitzer Prize for Commentary in May 2020 for her 1619 Project essay that was full of historical inaccuracies and diatribes against the United States of America. But then again, why shouldn't we be surprised when a *New York Times* "Beyoncé" journalist wins a Pulitzer? Didn't the *New York Times* Moscow correspondent Walter Duranty, "The Stalin of Journalism," win a Pulitzer in 1932 for his Soviet propaganda campaign that denied the mass starvation of Ukrainians by Joseph Stalin? The *Times* knew all along that Duranty was lying, just as they know today about the historical malpractice of their and Jones' 1619 Project.

The 1619 Project presents American history completely through the lens of race, slavery, and white supremacy. Its goal is to "reframe the country's history, understanding 1619 as our true founding, and places the consequences of slavery and the contributions of black Americans at the very center of the story we tell ourselves about who we are."

Hannah Jones' 1619 Project Pulitzer-winning essay declares that "Anti-black racism runs in the very DNA of this country," and that it was birthed in the blood of white supremacy and slavery in 1619. Thus, it defines America as a racist nation not built on the wonderful republican ideas of equality, liberty, and free enterprise for all, but on the persecution and oppression of all black people.

According to 1619 Project, the most egregious of the white man's sins was his 1776 revolutionary design by the white slave-owing Founding Fathers to stop Great Britain from abolishing slavery, and not the "white" interpretation that says the American Revolution was about freedom from the imperial yoke of the British Empire. This bogus claim, with no evidence whatsoever, was denounced by many of the most eminent scholars of U.S. history, many of whom reside on the left side of the political spectrum. Black American Leslie M. Harris of Northwestern University, an American historian and an expert in African American studies, in an article in Politico titled "I Helped Fact-Check the 1619 Project. The Times Ignored Me," responded to Hannah Jones' claim by saying, "Far from being fought to preserve slavery, the Revolutionary War became a primary disrupter of slavery in the North American colonies."

It is very relevant to note that the British slave trade and slavery would not be outlawed until 1807 and 1833, respectively. It took decades of parliamentary battles by black and white abolitionists and politicians such as the ex-slave Olaudah Equiano, MP William Wilberforce, Thomas Clarkson, Hannah More, and many more. The 1619 Project will not tell you that "black" African tribal chiefs were not happy with the "white" British Royal Navy for disrupting their lucrative slave trading.

Claremont Institute writer Charles Kesler wrote a column on June 19, 2020, titled "Call them the 1619 riots," in which he described the destruction of property across America and the destruction of presidential statues by BLM and others. Hannah Jones responded to the charge on Twitter by saying she "would be proud to be a part of the destruction" of American presidents such as George Washington and Thomas Jefferson. Jones shows us the real anti-American nature of the 1619 Project and its ultimate goal of dismantling our wonderful republic under God.

The essay to follow Hannah Jones was by Princeton sociologist Matthew Desmond. Do you remember how we began our discussion of 1619 Project advertising on Facebook and Twitter where they quote Dr. Desmond saying, "In order to understand the brutality of American capitalism you have to start on the plantation"? Desmond's 1619 Project essay cites plantation bookkeeping and concentrations of Southern "capital" as evidence that American capitalism had its beginnings in slavery.

Desmond wants you to believe that Southern slaveholders were "capitalists" because they were making "capital." What Desmond doesn't want you to know is that slavery had been around for thousands of years before so-called "capitalism" made money or riches for the slave owners. The Democratic Southern slave economy was the opposite of capitalism or free enterprise; it was an economy created on slave labor, not on free labor and free market enterprising.

The second generation of British abolitionists included Richard Cobden (1804–1865) and John Bright (1811–1889). They were not only passionate haters of slavery, but they were also strong advocates of free trade versus slave-plantation economics. John Bright was highly esteemed by Abraham Lincoln. It's relevant to point out that in the brilliant film *Lincoln* portrayed by the equally brilliant Oscar-winning actor Daniel Day Lewis, a photograph of the British statesman John Bright is on the left-hand corner of the mantelpiece of Lincoln's fireplace. The abolitionists Bright, Cobden, and many others were dedicated free-trade "capitalists" and staunch advocates of the classical liberal economics of Adam Smith and David Ricardo.

The pro-slavery advocate and anti-capitalist George Fitzhugh (1806–1881) from Virginia was considered the premier pro-slavery intellectual in Southern Democratic plantation circles and was widely read and quoted in their justification of an anti-free trade, pro-slave-society. In his books *Cannibals All! Or, Slaves without Masters* and *Sociology for the South, or, the Failure of Free Society*, Fitzhugh declares that the "Negro was but a grown up child" who needs slavery to take care of him, and that the Democratic slave South must throw such classic liberal economists as "Adam Smith, Say, Ricardo & Co., in the fire."

Fitzhugh also attacked John Locke's theory of social contract and called Thomas Jefferson's 1776 use of it in the Declaration of Independence as a heresy that fed "insidious individualism and capitalism." Fitzhugh argued in his 1854 *Sociology of the South* that free markets and free labor constituted a destructive system that must be replaced by a slave economy for poor whites and blacks, because it is the "very best form of socialism." According to Fitzhugh, plantation slave economics and sociology were "a beautiful example of communism, where each one receives not according to his labor, but according to his wants."

Princeton University American historian Allen Guelzo writes,

> The clinching refutation of the slavery-is-capitalism theory comes from the mouths of the slave owners themselves. They would have been aghast at the idea they were presiding over Yankee capitalism. Capitalism, complained slavery's paladin, John C. Calhoun, "operated as among the

efficient causes of that great inequality of property which prevails in most European countries. No system can be more efficient to rear up a moneyed aristocracy. Its tendency is, to make the poor poorer, and the rich richer."

It appears that the 1619 Project took their historical cues from the Marxist New History of Capitalism school of thought. Their anti-capitalistic critical theory distorts economic and historical data by extrapolating slavery as the foundation of Western capitalistic practice. They conflate the plantation slave system with laissez-faire economic enterprise while they ignore the inextricable relationship of classical liberal economists and abolitionism.

The 1619 Project idea that Southern plantation slavery created a "capitalistic economy" is an absurd notion with a profound misunderstanding of Economics 101. It is why the Southern slave states so feared free enterprise in the free Northern states. The free Northern states had a creative entrepreneurial spirit that exploded with enterprising creativity and productivity. It is why the North was such an economic giant compared to a plantation economy based on chattel slavery. Yes, Southern slave plantations had "capital," but it was not earned in the free market but off the backs of slave labor. Their "Cotton is King" slave economy was nothing in comparison to Northern free enterprise. The Southern slave economy had capital, but it was not capitalism. While cotton may have been king in the South, their slave economy kept most in the South poor while the Northern population grew more and more prosperous as Democratic slavery expanded in the South and West.

Visitors to America in the pre-Civil War years noticed the stark contrast between the free-trade North and the Southern slave economy. You would see the same contrast between the free-trade democratic countries of Western Europe after WWII and the Marxist slave economy of Soviet socialism in Eastern Europe or the slave socialism experienced in North Korea versus the free enterprise of democratic South Korea. Free enterprise is the inextricable partner and lifeblood of thriving liberal democracies and the antitheses of plantation and Marxist slavery.

On June 16, 2020, Democratic Senator Tim Kaine of Virginia, Hillary Clinton's vice presidential candidate in 2016, during a speech on the Senate floor, declared that the United States "created" and "didn't inherit slavery from anyone." Here's the full context:

> We need to do much more within the criminal justice system, but also within all of our systems to dismantle the structure of racism that our federal state and local governments carefully erected and maintained over centuries. We know a little bit about this in Virginia; the first African-Americans who entered to the English colonies came to Point Comfort, Virginia in 1619. They were slaves. They'd been captured against their will, but they landed in colonies that didn't have slavery. There were no laws about slavery in the colonies at that time. The United States didn't inherit slavery from anybody. We created it. It got created by the Virginia General Assembly and the legislatures of other states. It got created by the court systems in colonial America that enforced fugitive slave laws.

Kaine goes on to say,

> There was no law mandating slavery on our shores
> when African slaves came ashore in 1619. Did
> slavery already exist in the world? Of course. But
> not in the laws of colonial America at the time; we
> could have been a nation completely without the
> institution. But colonial legislatures and courts,
> and eventually the U.S. legal system, created the
> institution on our shores and maintained slavery
> until the 13th Amendment. As I said, we didn't
> inherit it. We chose to create it.... We created it,
> and we created it and maintained it over centuries,
> and in my lifetime, we have finally stopped some
> of those practices, but we've never gone back to
> undo it, stopping racist practices at year 350 of 400
> years, but then taking no effort to dismantle them,
> is not the same as truly combating racism. But I'm
> mindful of the challenge laid down by our young
> people. No more politics as usual.

There is a lot going on in Democrat Senator Kaine's two-
minute speech that reflects the worldview and Democratic
political agenda of the 1619 Project, as well as BLM
Marxists, for that matter. Kaine is a strong advocate of
the 1619 Project and is a BLM supporter. Throughout his
speech, you can see the words and ideas of Hannah Jones
and 1619 Project and BLM Marxist ideology.

He starts with African slaves being brought to Virginia in
1619 and then says the United States didn't inherit slavery
but created it and maintained it over centuries, and we have
a duty today to "dismantle the structure of racism that our

federal state and local governments carefully erected and maintained over centuries."

This is, in a nutshell, the argument of 1619 Project and BLM. The problem is that while they rightfully bring up the horrors of chattel slavery—something I have been teaching and speaking about for over 40 years—they skip over key historical events and brave personalities that hated slavery and fought to end it even before 1776. They cherry pick historical events to reinforce their 1619 white "original sin" narrative versus the universal 1776 proclamation that all men are created equal.

The American side of slavery is not the only one. Those Virginian African slaves who arrived to America's shores in 1619 were originally from the Kingdom of Ndongo—modern Angola—where they were enslaved by the Imbangala, an African warrior-cannibalistic tribe. Along with other African tribes such as the Ambaquista, they were able to "earn a good income" working with Portuguese slave traders.

African-on-African enslavement is a historical fact ignored or minimized by the 1619 Project and by many in the lefty world of "blame the white guy" for the "original sin" of slavery. The majority of the captured slaves brought to America were from Angola, Congo, Gambia, Senegal, and eastern Nigeria. European slave traders needed immense help from Africans to acquire their slaves. They needed help to locate, capture, and deliver the slaves, and many African chiefs were more than willing to help out.

Nat Amarteifio, a former mayor of Accra, Ghana, says, "There is still a willful amnesia about the role we [Africans] played in the slave trade." Unlike the 1619 Project and many in academia, some lefty newspapers have dealt with this "amnesia" as can be seen in articles including the *Washington Post*'s published on January 29, 2018, "An African country [Benin] reckons with its history of selling slaves"; and the *Guardians*' November 18, 2009, article, "African chiefs urged to apologize for slave trade."

Thriving on the sale of "black" slaves to "white" European slave traders, the Kingdom of Dahomey (present-day Benin) became a major center of the Atlantic slave trade. It prospered from 1732 until 1852 when the "white" British Navy put a naval blockade to stop the illegal slave trade due to laws passed by "white" British and American leaders. African King Adandozan (1798–1818), who increased slave raiding and the slave trade for the Kingdom of Dahomey, was furious when the "white" President Thomas Jefferson signed the U.S. Federal Act Prohibiting Importation of Slaves in 1807.

It was the African King Ghezo (1818–1858) of Dahomey who was upset with the "whites" of Great Britain and their "white" Royal Navy for diminishing his involvement in the Atlantic slave trade. Slaves were still arriving in the Democratic white south up to July 1860, as the last slave ship *Clotilda* from Dahomey, sent by African King Glele (1858–1889), arrived in Mobile, Alabama, with 110 to 160 slaves on board. Northern whites were furious with Southern whites and African black slave raiders and traders for this deplorable violation of "white" American and international law.

This is not to minimize the horror of black slavery in America or to exonerate white European slave traders, but it is to give us a broader context to the full black and white story of slavery in the United States of America. Like all nations, America is full of the good, the bad, and the ugly when it comes to the age-old struggle to be free.

The United States didn't create slavery; it was around for thousands of years before the first African slaves landed in America in 1619. We have historical records of slavery in Mesopotamia in 6800 B.C. In the 1700s B.C., Egyptians enslaved the Israelites, creating the famous phrase by Moses in Exodus 5:1: "Let my people go!" That phrase and the Exodus story of Passover, when the Jews fled Egyptian slavery, were used by abolitionists in England and America in the 1800s and by civil rights activists in the 1950s and 60s.

The Greeks, from the Spartans to the Athenians, relied on the slave labor of captives. In the ancient Roman world, one in three of the population of Italy was a slave, and one in five across the Empire. African tribal slavery was commonplace for well over a thousand years, and by the 8th century A.D., African slaves were a common part of the world of Islam. It has been estimated that there were more slaves in India than in the entire Western world. China, during the era of common place slavery, has some of the world's largest slave markets. German tribes had captured so many slaves in conquest that they created the world "slave" from *Slav* after the Slavic tribes they conquered. English philosopher John Stuart Mill observed, "Almost every people now civilized have consisted, in majority, of slaves."

Slavery existed long before 1619, contrary to what is commonly assumed in today's lefty politically correct culture that it was the "original sin" of the United States. The whole human race sinned when it came to the matter of slavery, and in reality, it was the United States of America that was one of the first nations to realize it was morally wrong and took action to stop it.

In 1864, when President Lincoln wrote a letter to newspaper editor A.G. Hodges, it was a summary of a conversation he had with Hodges, former Senator Archibald Dixon, and Kentucky Governor Bramlette. Bramlette had protested the recruitment of a black regiment in Kentucky. In this letter Lincoln wrote,

> I am naturally anti-slavery. If slavery it not wrong, nothing is wrong.... If God now wills the removal of a great wrong, and wills also that we of the North as well as you of the South, shall pay fairly for our complicity in that wrong, impartial history will find therein new cause to attest and revere the justice and the goodness of God.
> Yours truly, A. Lincoln

When Democrat Senator Tim Kaine says, "We could have been a nation completely without the institution" of slavery, his partial, partisan, biased 1619 Project history ignores the slave history of his own Democratic Party, his own Democratic slave state of Virginia, and the very multi-layered and complex history of abolition in America. When Senator Kaine's Democratic Party declares in the "Our History" section of their DNC website that "For more than 200 years, our Party has led the fight for civil rights," he knows that, like the 1619 Project, it is a lie and not "impartial history." The Democratic Party is working hard to control the past to control future voters of America.

When President Lincoln called slavery "the great wrong," he was expressing an idea that was not universal in 1864. Lefty academia today may condemn slavery as the great "original sin" of white America, but what is the black and white story for life, liberty, and equality in America? That is our next journey.

Chapter 7

1776 American History in Black and White

The word *liberty* has its origin in the Greco-Roman world. The Latin word *"liber"* or "the free one" was politically defined in Roman law as *"liber homo"* or "a freeman being in a state of independence from another's arbitrary will." According to the Greek concept of liberty, "to be free" was to not to have a master in relationship to slavery. Thus, liberty had a contra-distinctive relationship to slavery and was inextricably woven into the concept of "freedom and equality."

Fast forward to 1776 and the "American War for Life and Liberty," otherwise called the American Revolution. Through the Continental Congress and its Committee of Five, Thomas Jefferson, accepting feedback and help from John Adams and Benjamin Franklin and observing the political theory of John Locke and Algernon Sydney, declared to the world, "We hold these truths to be self-evident, that all men are created equal."

The brilliant Roman Catholic English philosopher G.K. Chesterton observed, "America is the only nation in the world that is founded on a creed ... that creed is set forth in the Declaration of Independence." Created equal! What a revolutionary universal declaration. All men— ALL humanity everywhere—are created equal. Our 1776 Continental Congressmen were willing to put their "lives, fortunes and sacred honor" on the line for life and liberty from the tyranny and slavery of the STATE.

Unfortunately, hypocrisy and a double standard existed when it came to liberty and equality for all. In 1776, many of our Founders knew that as they declared for liberty and equality, the reality of slavery was a profound contradiction to their universal declaration.

Yes, 1619 Project, you are correct to teach and preach on that hypocrisy, as I do. But I believe you miss the mark about the wonder of our 1776 universal proclamation of liberty and equality for all that so moved Frederick Douglass and Martin Luther King Jr. they called it "wise and magnificent."

Douglass and King understood that the seedbed of equality for all was planted deeply in the American soil and soul by even those who owned slaves at the time, believing that someday soon that pernicious and vile institution would be eradicated from the land.

We know that before the Civil War of 1861–1865, the federal government and state governments were all over the place when it came to liberty and slavery. The federal government of 1787–1789 understood the profound and inextricable bond between the 1787 Constitution, the 1789 Bill of Rights, and the 1776 Declaration of Independence, which declared that "ALL men were created equal." The last sentence of the 1787 Constitution reads, "In the Year of our Lord one thousand seven hundred and eighty seven and of the Independence of the United States of America the Twelfth..."

Why did our Founders put in "the Twelfth" into our Constitution? It's quite simple: they saw life, liberty, and "equality for all" as the origin of the Union of the United States of America as beginning in 1776, which they sought to make "more perfect." To our Founders "equality for all" was the very essence of liberty from tyrannical government, whether it was at the federal or state level.

But our Founders also knew that they had a problem with that wonderful concept of equality for all: that problem was SLAVERY. As slavery was flourishing around the world in 1776 (93–95% of the trans-Atlantic slave trade went to South America, Cuba, and the Caribbean Islands), even Great Britain was not dealing with eradicating slavery. Many of our Founders saw the blatant contradictions of preaching liberty and equality while maintaining slavery.

Founder George Mason, a fourth-generation Virginian slave owner, was conflicted about the obvious contradiction and believed slavery would bring "the judgment of heaven" upon America. As early as 1765, Mason wrote that the practice of slavery was immoral and it undermined the character of a free people. Time and time again, George Mason said that slavery "is daily contaminating the minds and morals of our people." He was right to speak out but wrong to continue as a slave owner until he died in 1792.

The eminent American Revolution historian Bernard Bailyn, still alive at age 97, contends that the idea of abolition, unfortunately, was not in full swing in 1776 and was a gradual movement in America. In his book, *Faces of Revolution: Personalities and Theme in the Struggle for American Independence*, he writes, "What is significant in the historical context of the time is not that the liberty loving revolutionaries allowed slavery to survive, but that they—even those who profited directly from the institution—went so far in condemning it, confining it, and setting in motion the forces that would ultimately destroy it."

The American Revolution brought an awareness of the contradiction of slavery and liberty living side by side in the same land. It was our Founders who laid the foundation for the termination of slavery within a few generations, leading to the "Second American Revolution," our Civil War, which was dedicated to the proposition that all men are created equal.

During the summer of 2020 George Floyd riots, the statues of a number of our Founding Fathers were desecrated or destroyed. On June 18th, 2020, in Portland, Oregon, BLM activists toppled a President Washington statue and spray-painted "You're on Native Land," "BLM," and "1619." I wonder where they got the idea to put "1619" on the President Washington statue. In that same city at Jefferson High School, a BLM crowd of about 1,000 toppled a statue of the school's namesake, President Thomas Jefferson. Why? Because he was a white guy who owned slaves.

While it is true Jefferson owned slaves, he, like George Mason of Virginia, believed it was a "moral depravity." Inscribed on the Jefferson Memorial are his words,

> God who gave us life gave us liberty. Can the liberties of a nation be secure when we have removed a conviction that these liberties are the gift of God? Indeed I tremble for my country when I reflect that God is just, that His justice cannot sleep forever. Commerce between master and slave is despotism. Nothing is more certain written in the book of fate than that these people are to be free.

Abraham Lincoln used Jefferson's words many times in his fight against slavery before and during the Civil War.

During his first terms in the Virginia legislature, Jefferson proposed legislation to end slavery in his state. He was soundly defeated. He was constantly trying to find ways of getting legislation passed to end slavery in Virginia, but he was defeated every time. In 1806, as president of the United States, Jefferson promoted legislation to end the slave trade—an idea he had promoted since the 1770s—and on March 2, 1807, President Jefferson sign into law the "Act Prohibiting Importation of Slaves." As of January 1, 1808, it was illegal to import slaves into America.

Yes, Thomas Jefferson owned slaves, and that is a sad fact of history, but it is also a glad fact of history that in all of his hypocrisy, he did act upon to some degree his desire to see that "all men were created equal."

Many liberty-loving black patriots fought in the American Revolution. Crispus Attucks, who was of African and Native

American descent, was the first person killed in the Boston massacre and became a hero of the anti-slavery movement of the mid-19th century. (For those who say Attucks wasn't "black," I'd remind you that Barack Obama's mother was white, and yet he was considered black by most, with a few exceptions such as Morgan Freeman.) Peter Salem, a freed slave, fought bravely in the Continental Army at the battle of Concord on April 19, 1775, and again on June 17, 1775, at the Battle of Bunker Hill. He fought with other free black American patriots such as Seymour Burr, Alexander Aims, Cato Howe, Titus Coburn, Salem Poor, Phillip Abbot, Barzillai Lew, and others who fought for the dream of freedom in America. Oliver Cromwell and Prince Whipple, depicted in the famous German American Emanuel Leutze's 1851 painting of *Washington Crossing the Delaware*, were two brave black soldiers who served with General George Washington and other Americans generals during the American Revolution.

There were many anti-slavery Founders such as John Adams, Samuel Adams, Stephen Hopkins, Benjamin Rush, Elbridge Gerry, James Wilson, Benjamin Franklin, John Witherspoon, and John Jay. The Founding Father John Jay (1745–1829) was not only one the writers of *The Federalist Papers*, second governor of New York, and the first Chief Justice of the Supreme Court, but he was also the founder and president of the New York Manumission Society in 1785. This society, made up entirely of white men, one being Alexander Hamilton, battled against the slave trade, fought for the abolition of slavery, and created the African Free School for the poor and orphaned children of slaves and "free people of color."

Although John Jay's father, Peter Jay, was one of the largest slave owners in New York, John is a classic example of the development of the gradual evolution of Americans into the abolition camp. As governor of New York in 1799, he signed the "Act for the Gradual Abolition of Slavery."

The revolutionary liberty and equality rhetoric of 1776 caused the heroic black patriot Prince Whipple and 18 other free blacks in 1779 to send a petition to the New Hampshire legislature, declaring that slavery "was incompatible with justice, humanity and the rights of mankind." After the American Revolution, many Northern states such as New Hampshire (1779), Pennsylvania (1780), Massachusetts (1783), Rhode Island (1784), and Connecticut (1784) all explicitly said slavery could not be contained in their constitutions, and they adopted immediate or gradual legislative abolition plans or had their courts declare slavery unconstitutional.

Between 1776 and 1787, slavery in Northern states was dying or outlawed, while in the Southern states, it was flourishing and expanding with more and more legislation to ensure that effect. Our Northern Founders, as well as a number of Southern Founders such as James Madison, George Mason, Thomas Jefferson, and George Washington, desired to see it end, but they knew they needed to compromise with the Southern slave states to pass or ratify the Constitution to create our republic under God.

In 1789, following the ratification of the Constitution, the first federal Congress expanded its fight to end slavery by passing of the Northwest Ordinance. It was signed by President George Washington who stated, "I can only say that there is not a man living who wishes more sincerely than I do to see a plan adopted for the abolition of slavery." George Washington freed all his slaves in his 1799 will. Washington's plan, along with the first Congress, was to stop the expansion of slavery. Thus, their Northwest Ordinance outlawed slavery in the new territories, which in turn led to the creation of the free states of Ohio, Indiana, Illinois, Minnesota, Michigan, and Wisconsin.

Unfortunately, in 1793, the second federal Congress passed the Fugitive Slave Act, which was signed by President Washington. It gave power to local governments in both slave and free states to seize and return escaped slaves to their owners. It also imposed penalties on those who helped in their escape. It is relevant to note that one of President Washington's slaves, Oney Judge, escaped his household in 1796 at the age of 20. She lived in New Hampshire free until she died in 1848 at the age of 75. While Washington did use newspaper ads to find her and finally located her in New Hampshire, he decided not to litigate under the Fugitive Slave Act.

Oney remained free in New Hampshire, marrying a free black sailor and converting to Christianity. When the *Granite Freeman*, an abolitionist newspaper, interviewed Oney in 1847, they asked her if she ever regretted leaving the "easier life" as President Washington's slave to live a much harder life of poverty and labor. She declared, "No! I am FREE, and have I trust, been made a child of God by the means." Her story is an amazing universal and American story of the soul's desire to be free, and it should be taught in our schools as I have done for years.

As you can see, the federal government and our early presidents were all over the place between the advocacy of liberty versus the evils of slave tyranny. Gradually, Southern slave states, along with a Democratic-controlled Congress, reversed the 1789 federal prohibition of slavery in the territories. In fact, they successfully advanced slavery with the federal Missouri Act of 1820. Missouri entered the USA as a slave state and Maine as a free state. While they called it a "compromise," in reality, the federal government was complicit in the advancement of slavery. Several states were subsequently admitted as slave states as the Democratic-controlled Congress ignored the freedom principles of our founding documents to promote slavery.

The sixth president of the United States, John Quincy Adams (1825–1829), the son of the second president John Adams (1797–1801), both of whom hated slavery, attacked Democratic duplicity by saying, "The first step of the slaveholder to justify by argument the peculiar institution [of slavery] is to deny the self-evident truths of the Declaration of Independence. He denies that all men are created equal. He denies that they have inalienable rights."

John Quincy was a "white" guy speaking out against Democratic "white" guys who supported the preservation and advancement of slavery. The reality is that the 1619 Project story of American history is much more complicated than all "white guys"—are evil narrative. When John Quincy Adams was a Massachusetts congressman (1830–1848), he was nicknamed "the hell-hound of slavery" for relentlessly speaking out against it. The frustrated and angry Democratic-controlled Congress passed a "gag rule" to shut up Adams and other non-Democrats for speaking out against slavery on the Congressional House floor. So much for freedom of speech and debate, Democrats.

Through the influence of the young Democratic Party, Southern states invoked their state sovereignty to work around the 1808 federal law that terminated the slave trade by passing more and more state laws protecting slavery. Eventually, Democrats controlled not only Southern state governments and used that power to preserve slavery, but they also began to have a profound influence on the federal government from 1830 to 1860 and used that power to advance slavery.

In 1850, the Democratic-controlled federal government passed a modified and more egregious version of the 1793 Fugitive Slave Act, so that slaves could not testify on their own behalf. Also, federal commissioners and agents were used to force Northern states to return escaped slaves. The federal government was, in reality, kidnapping free black Americans. Democrats who earlier in the name of "states' rights" were fighting for slavery were now hypocritically denying and violating Northern "states' rights" to stop slavery.

By 1854, federal government Democrats passed the Kansas-Nebraska Act, which advanced slavery into the new territories. Then in 1857, the Democratic-controlled Supreme Court passed the dreadful 1857 Dred Scott decision, declaring that black slaves were not citizens or persons but were equal to property such as pigs and cows.

The Democratic Party platforms of 1840, 1844, 1848, 1852, 1856, and 1860 contained an explicit defense of slavery in the name of "the liberal principles embodied by Jefferson in the Declaration of Independence, and sanctioned in the Constitution, which makes ours the land of liberty." Land of liberty Democrats? Right. Tell that lie to the slave. It is why in Frederick Douglass' 1853 speech titled "The Slavery Party," he declared, "The best representation of the slavery party in politics is the Democratic Party." Douglass remained a dedicated lifelong Republican and freedom fighter.

Southern Democratic politicians reflected their party platform by declaring in their speeches or legislation the "positive good of slavery." In 1836, Congressman James Henry Hammond from South Carolina, furious with white Northern abolitionists, gave an impassioned two-hour speech on the House floor defending the practice of slavery by saying, "Slavery is said to be evil ... but it is not evil. On the contrary, I believe it to be the greatest of all the great blessings which a kind Providence has bestowed upon our glorious region." When Hammond became the Democratic governor of South Carolina in 1842 and then a Democratic U.S. senator in 1857, he was a vociferous champion of the "positive good of slavery" and the "negative bad" of free labor and oppression by Northern capitalist owners. The 1619 Project does not separate Northern free enterprise from the slave economy of the South.

Besides the renowned slave philosopher of Virginia, George Fitzhugh (discussed earlier), and South Carolinian James Henry Hammond, the most famous slave-state philosopher for the South was South Carolina's John C. Calhoun. Calhoun's speeches and writings, such as his 1837 article, "Slavery a Positive Good," or his 1850 "Disquisition on Government," rejected John Locke's, Algernon Sidney's, and

Thomas Jefferson's Natural Law political theory of "equality for all." Calhoun's white supremacy political theory argued that the "Negro's nature is eternally inferior" and could never achieve equality with the "superior white man."

Calhoun disdained the *Federalist Papers* because he felt they argued against states' rights and for a federal constitutional republic that believed in equality for all. Calhoun desired to change our Constitution to perpetuate slavery in the states. While Calhoun died in 1850, his white supremacist/secessionist/racist ideas lived on in the Southern slave state legislatures, governors, and institutions before, during, and after the Civil War.

To the Democratic-Confederate political philosophers and politicians of the 1850s and 1860s, Abraham Lincoln's words at the 1863 Gettysburg Address were heresy and tyranny as he declared, "Four score and seven years ago our fathers brought forth on this continent, a new nation, conceived in liberty, and dedicated to the proposition that all men are created equal." Do the Lincoln math. Fourscore and seven equals 87; 1863 – 87 = 1776; 1776, the glorious year of our republic's birth!

Why was 1776 considered heresy by the Democrats? According to the Democratic white supremacy presupposition, Lincoln's Lockean-Jeffersonian worldview of equality for all did not begin in 1776 because the black man could never be equal to the white man. Lincoln begged to differ and understood that the road to liberty and equality for all was declared in 1776, the glorious year of the birth of a new nation, conceived in liberty and dedicated to the proposition that all men are created equal!

Lincoln keenly understood that our Founders argued from the moral precepts of a natural law tradition rooted in the Western civilization-Judeo-Christian worldview of Aristotle, Augustine, Aquinas, Locke, et al., that presumed the existence of a Creator God called in the Declaration of Independence "the Supreme Judge of the World."

Lincoln self-evidently knew that life, liberty, and equality derived from God; thus, it was the duty and purpose of our republic under God to fight to break the chains of Democratic Party slavery. It is interesting to note that in 1991, during the Senate confirmation hearings for Supreme Court justice nominee Clarence Thomas, in typical anti-natural law tradition, Democrat Senator Joe Biden attacked Judge Thomas' positive belief in God's natural law.

Lincoln's great legal mind understood that many of our liberty-loving Founders never conceived of a nation dedicated to slavery by government, because to do so would have been a profound contradiction and tyranny of the worse kind. The 1861 slave state Confederate republic was dedicated to the proposition that their new nation was conceived in slavery because the black man was inferior and not equal to the white man.

What Southern political theorists have failed to understand from Calhoun to Democratic Confederates such as Jefferson Davis and Alexander Stephens is that America was founded in 1776 on an idea. That idea is quite simple and profound at the same time: ALL men are created equal, and true liberty is a natural God-given right to be free from government harm and control *at any level of government.* The Southern slave-state secession argument was the antithesis of that self-evident truth. It was their fanatical white racial argument, under the guise of so-called "states' rights," that led to a bloody and avoidable Civil War. No slavery equals no secession, and thus no rebellious Civil War.

By 1860, not only had Southern states entrenched slavery in the South through Democratic state governments, but the federal government, controlled by Democrats, had also successfully advanced and entrenched slavery throughout the Southern and Western territories of the United States. Both state and federal governments were working hard to continue the enslavement of human beings. This was anti-liberty tyranny by both forms of government.

In 1854, in Ripon, Wisconsin (not too far from my hometown), a new political party, the Republican Party, composed of blacks and whites, men and women, was created and dedicated to the principles of authentic republicanism and to the proposition that all men are created equal. Of the nine planks of the 1856 Republican Party platform, seven of them directly dealt with civil rights and racial equality. Study their platforms, political speeches, and philosophy, and you will discover that their "liberty for all" ideas clearly separated them from the dominant Democratic Slave Party. The Democrats influenced the tyranny of the federal government and their Southern state governments over the natural God-given rights of all Americans, black and white.

The early principles of the Republican Party held that man's natural condition, based on Christian natural law, is freedom, and that the Constitution had an inextricable relationship to the Declaration of Independence that declared that all men are created equal. The Republican Party understood that through legal means they could influence the federal government to stop the advance of slavery from the territories to Washington D.C. and on the high seas. They, like Lincoln, had hoped to construct a "cordon of freedom" around the slave states that would gradually strangle slavery, hopefully convincing the Southern slave states to peaceably abandon their pernicious institution.

It is important to remind the 1619 Project that it was white Republicans who were challenging the white supremacy of white Democrats. Northern white state legislators, white governors, and the white Supreme Court began to challenge white Democratic federal slave tyranny. White Southern states were offended that white Northern and white Western states "denounced as sinful the institution of slavery" and allowed for abolitionist societies to freely express their disdain for slavery and desire for it to vanish from America. Southern white postmasters refused to deliver Northern white abolitionist literature, and most Democratic slave states declared public anti-slavery speeches a criminal offense. The Democratic South was not defending "states' rights" and limited republican government against a tyrannical federal government; it was defending white supremacy over their black slaves at all government levels.

I stress this "white-on-white" historical dynamic to illustrate the absurd notion by the 1619 Project, the Zinn Project, BLM, and many lefty academics of their anti-American lopsided presentation of the oppressive world of the white man in America. There are far too many to mention, but one such righteous white warrior was ex-Democrat turned Republican Charles Sumner of Massachusetts.

Senator Sumner had a reputation as the denouncer of "Slavocracy" or the power by Democratic slave owners over the U.S. Federal government in the 1840s and 1850s. On May 19 and 20, 1856, in response to the Democratic Kansas-Nebraska Act, which advanced slavery, Senator Sumner gave a passionate speech attacking Democratic slavery. Two days later, following the speech, a Democratic representative from South Carolina, Preston Brooks, went from the House and on the Senate floor proceeded to beat Sumner senseless, almost killing him. It took three and a half years for Senator Sumner to recover, and when he did and gave his first speech on June 4, 1860, he unabashedly attacked "The Barbarism of Slavery." This white Republican was attacking white Democratic slavocracy. It was not the pigmentation of Senator Sumner's skin that made his battle moral; it was the righteous 1776 republican liberty idea behind it.

The Democratic South did not rebel against the federal government in 1860 and 1861 to advance "republicanism, equal protection of equal rights, and government by consent within its boundaries; it seceded to secure the Southern way of life, a way of life that revolved in many ways around the institution of human slavery." Democratic Southern so-called "states' rights" advocates ignored the inextricable connection between republicanism, justice, equality, and freedom of expression.

The election of Republican Abraham Lincoln in November of 1860 was the last straw for the Democratic slave-state apostles of disunion and slavery. Even before Lincoln was sworn in as president of the United States, when he was just a citizen with no executive power, the Democratic Southern slave states took action. Their words, speeches, decrees, commissions, and Calhounian "slavery as a positive good" argumentation had won the day.

How ironic that the Democratic Southern slave states were content in the 1850s when the federal government supported the slave states' philosophy and practice, but the moment an anti-slavery Republican was elected to the federal position of president in 1860, they declared "Secession!" Let's look at the inextricable thinking of the slave states between slavery, state power, white supremacy, and true liberty. The key time period is from 1860 to 1861.

The Democratic Convention, held during April and May 1860 in South Carolina, saw many slavery Democrats upset that too many moderate Democrats were supporting Stephen Douglas who, while supporting slavery, wanted to leave it up to election results; in other words, "moderate" Democrats wanted the "freedom" to vote for slavery. The slave state advocates, not willing to compromise on slavery, opened the door for the election of the Republican Abraham Lincoln. Once that occurred, slave state defenders defied the legal and democratic process of a presidential election and turned their wrath on what they called "Negro Republicans," "Black Republicans," and the "Black Party of Lincoln."

These Southern slave state advocates never separated "black" Abraham Lincoln from the "black" Republican Party. Democratic Southern slave state thinking equated "white" Abraham Lincoln and the Republican Party as one and the same "black" entity that was hell bent on destroying their "heavenly" slave state plantation society.

Not liking that the people had spoken in the election of 1860, the Democratic Southern slave states began to organize an illegal and rebellious secession from the USA. In the process, they argued, articulated, and disseminated slave-state secessionist ideas all throughout the South, with South Carolina leading the charge. As Democratic slave states left the United States, they explained why they did. The *PRIMARY* reason for secession was their desire to preserve and perpetuate slavery in their states and beyond. They mandated that any new state desiring to join their "new slave state republic," or CSA, the Confederate States of America, would have to endorse slavery; equality and liberty for all be damned!

After the election of Republican Abraham Lincoln in November of 1860, Southern slave states created secession commissioners to travel throughout the South to reinforce their slave state secession argument and to convince vacillating border states that the defense of slavery was worth the cause to confederate.

From Alabama to Mississippi to South Carolina and Georgia, the choice for the South was self-evidently clear that "this new union with Lincoln Black Republicans and free Negroes without slavery; or slavery under our old constitutional bond of union, without Lincoln Black Republicans, or free Negroes either, to molest us" must be fought against with secession if Southerners were to avoid "submission to Negro equality."

Common terminology used by Democratic Southern slave state secessionists and commissioners varied from Lincoln Negroes, Lincoln Black Republicans, Black Republicans, Black Republican Party, Negro Republican Platform, and Lincoln Negro Republicans. In their Democrat white supremacist worldview, the "election of the Negro Lincoln Republican" led to the denigration and subjugation of the white man, and that would inevitably lead to the "annihilation of the white race by Lincoln Republican Negroes." Notice the Democratic language 1619 Project! White Republicans were called black. Teach this in our schools and put this in the curriculum!

On Christmas Eve of 1860, South Carolina wrote a "Declaration of the Immediate Causes Which Induce and Justify the Secession of South Carolina from the Federal Union." In their list of causes were their grievances that Northern states were exercising their right to defy the Federal Fugitive Slave Act, and that Northern and Western states should not have the right to let abolitionists assemble and to speak out freely against slavery. So much for states' rights by the so-called Southern states' rights advocates. It was not about "rights"; it was always about power to enslave. We must always remember that states don't have rights. They have power, and that power is to be used to protect the God-given rights of all of its citizens.

When you study the Southern slave states' Declarations of Secession, you find over and over again attacks on Northern free states and the election of Abraham Lincoln, and a defense of "sister slave-holding states." From Texas to Virginia, Georgia, and Mississippi, you see the advancement of the inextricable relationship of white supremacy over the "inferior Negro race" and slavery's inextricable relationship to states' rights.

The February 1, 1861, the Texas Declaration of Secession declared,

> We hold as undeniable truths that the governments of the various States, and of the confederacy itself, were established exclusively by the white race, for themselves and their posterity; that the African race had no agency in their establishment; that they were rightfully held and regarded as an inferior and dependent race, and in that condition only could their existence in this country be rendered beneficial or tolerable. That in this free government all white men are and of right ought to be entitled to equal civil and political rights; that the servitude of the African race, as existing in these States, is mutually beneficial to both bond and free.

In late 1860 and early 1861, the Southern slave state mindset was to defend secession as the only viable way to survive the world of "Black Lincoln Republicans," and if rebelling and going to war against the United States of America was necessary for the survival of the Democrat white race, then so be it. This was a war of white Democrats versus liberty-loving black and white Republicans.

On March 11, 1861, the Constitution of the Confederate States was created. While copying much from our 1787 federal Constitution, it purged all compromises with slavery and created an explicitly pro-slavery and anti-liberty slave republic document. On March 21, 1861, in Savannah,

Georgia, the vice president of the Confederacy, Alexander Stevens, proudly declared in his infamous and anti-liberty "Confederate Cornerstone Speech":

> Our Confederate Republic ... is passing through one of the greatest revolutions in the annals of the world. Seven States have within the last three months thrown off an old government and formed a new.... Our new government is founded upon exactly the opposite idea; its foundation are laid, its cornerstone rests, upon the great truth that the negro is not equal to the white man; that slavery, subordination to the superior race, is his natural and normal condition. This, our new government, is the first, in the world, based upon this great physical, philosophical, and moral truth.

Thus, the Democratic CSA started their rebellious Civil War versus the federal government to secure their slave republic by attacking the federal Fort Sumter on April 12, 1861. To preserve slavery, the liberty-defying and Constitution-denying Democratic slave states joined illegally into a confederation, alliance, and compact in open rebellion against the United States of America.

Because they did not get their way at the polls, a disgruntled minority violated their sacred oath to uphold the rules of the U.S. Constitution. On May 5, 1789, the Senate passed its first bill—the Oath Act. That first oath, for members and civil servants, was very simple: "I do solemnly swear that I will support the Constitution of the United States." In Article 6, Section 3, of the Constitution, it clearly states that "The states shall be bound by oath or affirmation to support this Constitution." They swore under oath to be part of the Union forever. By illegally and unconstitutionally seceding to preserve slavery, they were breaking their constitutional oath.

Additionally, Article 1, Section 10, limits state power by stipulating, "No State shall enter into any Treaty, alliance, or Confederation.... No State shall, without the Consent of Congress ... keep Troops, or Ships of War in times of Peace, enter into any agreement or compact with another State, or with a foreign Power, or engage in War, unless actually invaded."

In 1861, in violation of the federal Constitution, a domestic enemy—the unconstitutional, illegal and tyrannical CSA or Confederate States of America—initiated and engaged in an offensive war against the United States of America to perpetuate the enemy of Liberty, SLAVERY.

Before Abraham Lincoln was even in office, the domestic enemy—the slave republic Louisiana—seceded from the Union on January 26, 1861. That same day, rebel forces plotted the seizure of the New Orleans Mint. The secretary of the United States Treasury warned that "if anyone attempts to haul down the American flag, shoot him on the spot." Disregarding this command, the New Orleans Mint superintendent, William A. Elmore, resigned from federal employment, and the Mint was taken over in the name of the State of Louisiana. Elmore and other mint employees, including Treasurer A. J. Guirot, Assayer Howard Millspaugh, and Dr. M. F. Bozano, retained their former jobs after violating their oath as federal officials to uphold the U.S. Constitution. In treasonous fashion, they swore allegiance to the Democratic Confederacy. Democratic domestic enemy Georgia, following Louisiana's rebellious example, illegally transferred its federal mint over to the central government of the Confederacy.

This aggressive, illegal rebellion occurred before the so-called first shots of the Civil War were heard. The Democratic Confederate aggressive/offensive war to preserve slavery started well before Lincoln was in office and before they fired the first shots on Fort Sumter on April 12, 1861.

While the slave state Democrats may have couched their secession with the rhetoric of freedom, they were in reality calling for the freedom to enslave, not to liberate. They were not acting in the liberty-loving Spirit of 1776 but in the slavery-loving Spirit of 1861. The Democratic slavery secession of 1861 was not a legitimate liberty-loving revolution in the Spirit of 1776 but a tyrannical anti-constitutional rebellion hell bent on the preservation and perpetuation of slavery. To quote Dr. Larry Schweikart in his excellent work, *A Patriot's History of the United States*, "It is not an exaggeration to say that the Civil War was about slavery and, in the long run, only about slavery."

The 1854 Republican Party's vision was to finish the job a number of our Founders started in 1776. Republican Abraham Lincoln not only had a brilliant legal mind but also saw within the Democratic liberty slavery argument a profound inconsistency. He also recognized the perversion of language by the Confederate slave republic in relationship to their use of the word *liberty*. In his "Wolf and Sheep" speech given in Baltimore, Maryland, in April 1864, his biblically literate audience would have known of the parable of the Good Shepherd from the Gospel of John when Lincoln said,

> We all declare for liberty; but in using the same *word* we do not all mean the same *thing*. With some the word liberty may mean for each man to do as he pleases with himself, and the product of his labor; while with others the same word may mean for some men to do as they please with other men, and the product of other men's labor. Here are two, not only different, but incompatible things, called by the same name—liberty. And it follows that each of the things is, by the respective parties, called by two different and incompatible names— liberty and tyranny.

> The shepherd drives the wolf from the sheep's throat, for which the sheep thanks the shepherd as a *liberator*, while the wolf denounces him for the same act as the destroyer of liberty, especially as the sheep was a black one. Plainly the sheep and the wolf are not agreed upon a definition of the word liberty.

Abraham Lincoln understood plainly that the wolves of the Democratic slave republic defined *liberty* to meet their appetite for black sheep slave labor on their plantations. Lincoln equally understood that true liberty and equality for all could never be achieved in a nation half slave and half free. Lincoln understood, as Patrick Henry did, that sometimes liberty comes at the price of death. By 1864, hundreds of thousands of black and white Union soldiers had died to secure liberty for all.

Before Abraham Lincoln was assassinated by a white supremacist in April of 1865, Lincoln and the 118 Republicans in the House worked tirelessly to pass a constitutional amendment to abolish slavery—the 13th Amendment. All 118 Republicans voted for the amendment, and of the 82 Democrats, only 19 voted with the Republicans. After the Civil War, the Republicans were responsible for the passing of two more constitutional amendments: the 14th Amendment ending state discrimination, declaring, "Nor shall any State deprive any person of life, liberty, or property without due process of law"; and the 15th Amendment allowing all American males of age the right to vote. By the way, not one Democrat voted for the 14th and 15th Amendments.

For a few years after the Civil War, the former Confederates or Southern Democrats were not allowed to vote until they took a loyalty oath to the USA that respected the civil rights of black Americans. Many refused to take the oath, so the Republicans became the political majority in most of the Southern states. Subsequently, many blacks were elected to state legislatures. The first 42 blacks elected in Texas to the state legislature were all Republicans. In Alabama, the first 103 blacks elected to the state legislature were Republicans. In South Carolina, it was the first 190; in Mississippi, the first 112; in Florida, the first 30; in Virginia, the first 46; and in North Carolina, the first 30. In Georgia, 41 blacks were elected to the state legislature, and all were Republicans. Republican blacks were also elected to the federal government as senators and congressmen.

It was a wonderful sight to see in the South as black and white Republican legislators were working together to pass legislation to protect voting rights for blacks and to stop segregation in schools, public transportation, police, and many other institutions. Institutional systemic Democratic racism was slowly being destroyed by black and white Republicans in the late 1860s and early 1870s.

Unfortunately, once the Republicans left the South in the late 1870s, the Southern state governments became Democratic again and returned to their old tyrannical, racist ways and began to terrorize black and white Republicans through such Democratic organizations as the Ku Klux Klan, Red Shirts, and the Knights of White Camellia. Through vile "Jim Crow" laws, Democratic Southern state governments were able to defy the federal 14th and 15th Amendments, denying the life and liberty that so many blacks and whites had fought so hard for before, during, and after the Civil War.

These white supremacist systemic chains of racism were so entrenched into the institutions of the South and some parts of the North with their ugly "Sundown Towns" that they would not be broken until blacks and whites, Republicans and Democrats in the 1950s and 1960s challenged the bogus "states' rights" argument that violated the God-given rights of its black citizens. Blacks, whites, and others created federal laws such as the 1957 Civil Rights Act, 1960 Civil Rights Act, 1964 Civil Rights Act, 1965 Voting Rights Act, and 1968 Fair Housing Act; there were also important Supreme Court decisions from the 1954 *Brown v. Board of Education* to the 1967 *Loving v. Virginia*. These laws and decisions eradicated Democratic institutional racism that long plagued America.

The 1619 Project, the Zinn Education Project, the Black Lives Matter at School curriculum, activist media, and Democrats indoctrinate our youth that "America was founded on slavery and racism" whose legacy will always be with us. Senator Tim Kaine shouts that "America invented slavery." CNN media activist and BLM supporter Don Lemon declares, "If you grew up in America, you came out of American soil, considering the history of this country ... how can you not be racist?" They all distort reality and run roughshod over many of the facts of history with a cherry-picked agenda that insults millions of God-fearing Americans, black and white and every color in between, who were and are dedicated to the proposition that all men and women are created equal.

If we are to overcome their imbalanced bad and ugly narratives, it must be done through the presentation of the whole truth of American history in black and white, setting the record straight of our exceptionally glorious and good history along with our inglorious bad and ugly history.

Chapter 8

They Were There in 1776!

We need to pray for President Trump and our republic under God.

Antifa, BLM, the Democratic Party, the activist media *mobocrats*, and all leftists in between have taken to the airways and into the streets in their never-ending war to destroy life, liberty, and democracy in America. The 1619 Project, the Zinn Education Project, the Black Lives Matter at School curriculum, and many others continue with their bad and ugly narrative of the American story throughout our schools in this great land. This lefty Trojan horse education continues to spread its cancerous cultural Marxism into the hearts and minds of our youth.

Throughout the years of my teaching career, I have received a number of kudos from my students and former students. On Martin Luther King Jr. Day last year, I received an email from a student who said,

Hi Dr. J, I just wanted to let you know how much I appreciate and value everything I have learned in your classes, you have taught me such strong values and morals in the past 3 years.... You've been telling us in class over and over again how people in the world will attack us for our views and you are right I never thought I would get such a hard time from other students and even from my own family. I just want to thank you so much for instilling in me a love for God, this country, history and good values. For making me appreciate veterans, and people who are currently serving in the military. For giving me such a different outlook on life and for inspiring me to stand up for what I believe in. I also want to thank your mom and dad for raising you to become such an inspiring person, and your dad for fighting in WWII against tyranny. I can't wait for class tomorrow.

Yes, this email did make me cry. It humbled me and helped me see once again the vital importance of a positive and honest education. But every once in a while, I receive messages from my former students—usually while in college—that let me know how disappointed they are in me. They remind me what the university has done to our kids. One student wrote,

> You're out of your f%^*ing mind and you're a danger to the children you teach ... as soon as the baby boomers die off, so will the Republican party. So have fun on your pink cloud while it lasts. But know in the future everyone is going to be brown

and queer and agnostic and won't give a sh*t about anything you've done. You don't matter.

Another student, a graduate of the University of Minnesota, opined,

> To think that you were someone I used to look up to. I am disgusted. I hope your white privilege privileges you with eternal guilt, shame and well deserved shortcomings. You say that America is doomed because of how universities are "indoctrinating our youth"? America has and is experiencing many social, political, and economic disparities because U.S. citizens are not learning the truth of our country's history. America was built upon the white man's colonization of native lands and has continued to be ruled by perpetually imperialist viewpoints of white European men. America is doomed because the white population has never paused to reconcile with our own fault as well as make reparations for the travesty that we caused, and CONTINUE TO CAUSE to so many peoples of so many nations. We are doomed because nothing good can be built from the colonization and destruction of human beings. You were my history teacher, and that is why I am particularly upset with you, your views, and people like you and Trump. I learned nothing from you but lies. Your ignorance concerns me more than anything.

I have to admit these messages sting for a bit, but then I am reminded of the worldview war we are in, so I try to find the patience to respond both graciously and factually to the feelings of my former students. However, the facts of history, now more than ever, must be taught to confront the feelings of so many of our students who have been profoundly impacted and transformed by the cultural Marxism of their instructors. Let us pray that their feelings don't turn them into *mobocrat* participants in leftism's continuous war to destroy our great republic under God.

As a kid in the 1960s, I remember my dad and his friends, all WWII veterans, talking about their days fighting Imperial Japan or National Socialism. You could see in their faces the toll that sacrifice had taken on their souls, and yet they all loved America and instilled that love in me, too. I was raised on Jefferson and Madison streets in my hometown, and I went to James Madison Junior High. My high school mascot was a 1776 Patriot. My whole neighborhood was filled with WWII veterans, and we all had a patriotic love of America and freedom.

But something happened along the way starting in the 1960s. It began in the classroom and is now in our streets. It was an attitude of ingratitude toward those who sacrificed for freedom and developed into a radical revolutionary movement that is determined to dismantle our democratic republic. I, for one, will never stop telling the exceptional story of this exceptional nation under God. And if they come for me, so be it.

I used to teach a University of Wisconsin American government college course at the academy where I work. My supervising professor told me I had to stop calling our

Founding Fathers "Founding Fathers," because he said, "I wasn't there and they ain't my daddy."

I told him, "The Founding Fathers were my daddy, and I was there!" Now, before you judge me as a loony nut job, let me explain.

How many of you have seen the classic Christmas film *It's a Wonderful Life*? It was done by a good friend of President Reagan, the great Hollywood director Frank Capra. Capra was not an American by birth or blood. He tells the story that when his impoverished Sicilian family moved to America in 1903, and as their ship was passing by the Statue of Liberty, Frank's father, Salvatore Capra, full of excitement, enthusiastically yelled out to his six-year-old son: "Francesco-Cico never forget the light of Lady Liberty! That is the greatest light since the star over Bethlehem. That is the Light of Freedom—never forget that Freedom!"

Frank Capra never did as he became a naturalized American citizen, not through blood but through his heart and the law. Capra filled his movies with the love of America's greatness, exceptionalism, and the moral principles that can be shared by all as legal citizens of the United States of America.

Consider Capra's 1939 film, *Mr. Smith Goes to Washington*. It was released a month after the start of WWII and was banned by Nazi Germany. When the Nazis occupied France, they said their ban of the film would start in 30 days. One Parisian theater had it play every day for 30 days to sold-out crowds. Why? Because "Mr. Smith" in the film was dealing with the corruption of the government in Washington DC.

Mr. Smith, like Abraham Lincoln, whom Capra adored, is dedicated to the proposition that America is to be "of and by and for the people." So while *Mr. Smith Goes to Washington* was truly an American classic, it had a universal appeal that resounded with the love of individual liberty versus the corruption of state collectivism of, by, and for the government. In 1940, the French people, in the midst of dealing with the tyranny of Nazism, dreamed the dream of Mr. Smith's love of liberty.

So while Colin Kaepernick, Barack Obama, BLM, the 1619 Project, and leftist *mobocrats* absurdly declare that "racism is a part of our DNA that is passed on," and while they create bogus narratives of white privilege, white guilt by birth, and pigmentation politics by party, they defy and deny the reality and the sacrifice of those great freedom fighters throughout our history—regardless of color!

Those men and women—black and white and all colors in between—who were dedicated to the proposition that ALL are created equal and endowed by our Creator with the right to life, liberty, and equality, THEY were with our Founding Fathers in 1776!

When those six U.S. Marines raised Old Glory at Iwo Jima in 1945, and three of them never came home to their mothers, they were with our Founding Founders in 1776!

When our GIs died in the blood-soaked snow in the Battle of the Bulge in 1944, they were with our Founding Founders in 1776!

When the black American recipient of the Congressional Medal of Honor, William Carney, at the 1863 Civil War battle of Fort Wagner, grabbed Old Glory before she could hit the ground, while being hit with five Confederate bullets, and carried our republic's flag back to safety, he was with our Founding Founders in 1776!

When the black American Tuskegee Airmen shot down Nazi planes over Europe during WWII, they were with our Founding Fathers in 1776!

When the most decorated GIs in WWII, the American-Japanese Nisei, helped destroy Imperial Japanese oppression, they were with our Founding Fathers in 1776!

When my dad, "GI Joe Jacobs," in that PBY Catalina in 1945, helped stop Japanese terror in the Pacific, he was with our Founding Fathers in 1776!

Who fought and died for the 1865 13th Amendment to end slavery in America? Who fought for the 1868 14th Amendment that declares, "Nor shall any state deny any person of life, liberty, and property"? Who fought for the 1870 15th Voting Rights Amendment? Who fought for 1957, 1960, 1964, 1965, and 1968 Civil Rights Acts to end Jim Crow?

Dare I say it was Americans of ALL colors, of many heritages—African, Asian, European—Independents, Republicans, and Democrats who finally had the courage to stop the slavery and segregation of their party! This is the whole TRUTH, the good, and it must be taught before it is too late, in our classrooms and culture versus the tyranny and lies of cultural Marxism, political correctness, and anti-American indoctrination.

Every time I'm in Washington, D.C., I go to the Lincoln Memorial to pay homage to Martin Luther King Jr. and Abraham Lincoln. There is a plaque on the ground where Martin Luther King Jr. gave his wonderful August 28, 1963, "I Have a Dream" speech about fulfilling the "American dream" of freedom and equality for all. The last time I was there, I got on my knees and prayed on the plaque—at the very spot of the wonderful American Dream speech—and I thanked God for Martin Luther King Jr. and Abraham Lincoln and many others who fought to end systemic racism in America.

We have ended Democratic systemic racism in America, but there is a new prejudice that plagues America today. When King dreamed that one day his children would "not be judged by the color of their skin," I never imagined an America in which my children would be judged by the color of their skin and not by the content of their character and actions.

ALL lives should not be judged by the color of their skin and automatically assumed to be privileged, prejudiced, and guilty of thoughts, crimes, and actions they did not commit. We must all unite to stop the judgmental pigmentation politics that destroys the American dream of Rosa Parks, Coretta Scott King, Frederick Douglass, Ruby Bridges, Booker T. Washington, A. Philip Randolph, Roy Wilkins, Fannie Lou Hamer, Martin Luther King Jr., and so many more great Americans of ALL colors!

On September 3, 1894, Frederick Douglass delivered a speech titled "Blessings of Liberty and Education" at the Industrial School of Manassas in Manassas, Virginia. It was the 56th anniversary of his escape from slavery. During his speech, Douglass said, "I think colored people make a great mistake in saying so much of race and color. In this race-way they put the emphasis in the wrong place. The colored people should advance the high position of the Constitution. It makes no distinction on account of race or color, and they should make none."

During an interview with *60 Minutes* in 2005, Mike Wallace asked Morgan Freeman (I love his last name) about Black History Month. Freeman responded, "I don't want a Black History Month. Black history is American history."

Wallace retorted, "How are we going to get rid of racism until..."

Freeman interrupted and said, "Stop talking about it. I'm going to stop calling you a white man. And I'm going to ask you to stop calling me a black man. I know you as Mike Wallace. You know me as Morgan Freeman. You're not going to say, 'I know this white guy named Mike Wallace.' Hear what I'm saying?"

Do you hear what King, Douglass, and Freeman are saying, lefty *mobocrats*, BLM, 1619 Project, and Democratic Party?!

America needs to hear what they are saying. Black history is American history. It is our history in the struggle for freedom: the good, the bad, and the ugly. Enough of the divisive, dividing, and destructive anti-democratic rhetoric and actions that only focuses on color and the bad and the ugly. We need more *E pluribus unum*—"out of many, one"—and no more *Reductio ad Hitlerum*—all I disagree with are Nazis.

There is a small town near my hometown in Wisconsin named FREEDOM. Wisconsin was founded in 1848, and it was always a free state. A number of Southern black slaves escaped the Democratic South to Wisconsin to be free. One such slave was James Andrew Jackson. In 1830, he escaped the slave South to be free in Wisconsin. Jackson was one of the first settlers in the Freedom area, and when he was asked by the white township leaders if they could name their new town "Jackson," he said, "No, name it FREEDOM; this is where I found my freedom!" That is the essence of the American story in glory—a place to find freedom. Jackson became a dedicated Republican fighter for freedom, working with blacks and whites for the cause of life and liberty until the day he died.

This, too, is our calling until the day we die. Give us liberty or give us death!

Bibliography

Books

Bailyn, Bernard. *Faces of Revolution: Personalities & Themes in the Struggle for American Independence.* New York: Vintage Press, 1992.

Baldwin, Roger Nash. *Liberty under the Soviets.* New York: Vanguard Press, 1928.

Barton, David. *Setting the Record Straight: American History in Black & White.* Aledo: Wallbuilder Press, 2004.

Blight, David W. *Frederick Douglass: Prophet of Freedom.* New York: Simon & Schuster, 2018.

Bray, Mark. *Antifa: The Anti-Fascist Handbook.* Brooklyn: Melville House Publishing, 2017.

Brown, Timothy Scott. *Weimar Radicals: Nazis and Communists between Authenticity and Performance.* New York: Berghahn Books, 2009.

Cone, James H. *The Black Church and Marxism.* The Institute for Democratic Socialism, 1980.

_____. *Black Theology and Black Power.* New York: Orbis Books, 2018.

Flynn, Daniel. *Why the Left Hates America: Exposing the Lies That Have Obscured Our Nation's Greatness.* Roseville: Prima Publishing, 2002.

Fornieri, Joseph R. *The Language of Liberty*. Washington DC: Regnery Publishing, Inc., 2009.

Hill, Jason D. *We Have Overcome: An Immigrant's Letter to the American People*. New York: Bombardier Books, 2018.

Horowitz, David. *The Black Book of the American Left*. Los Angeles: Second Thoughts Books, 2017.

_____. *Dark Agenda: The War to Destroy Christian America*. West Palm Beach: Humanix Books, 2018.

_____. *The Shadow Party: How George Soros, Hillary Clinton, and the Sixties Radicals Seized Control of the Democratic Party*. Nashville: Thomas Nelson, 2006.

Josephus. *Antiquities of the Jews*. New York: First Rate Publishers, 1999.

Krannawitter, Thomas L. *Vindicating Lincoln: Defending the Politics of Our Greatest President*. Lanham: Rowman & Littlefield Publishing Company, 2008.

Kuehnelt-Leddihn, Erik von. *Leftism: From de Sade and Marx to Hitler and Marcuse*. New Rochelle: Arlington House, 1974.

Lindsay, James and Helen Pluckrose. *Cynical Theories: How Activist Scholarship Made Everything about Race, Gender, and Identity-and Why This Harms Everyone*. Durham: Pitchstone Publishing, 2020.

Loudon, Trevor. *The Enemies Within: Communists, Socialists and Progressives in the U.S. Congress.* Las Vegas: Pacific Freedom Foundation, 2013.

MacDonald, Heather. *The War on Cops: How the New Attack on Law and Order Makes Everyone Less Safe.* New York: Encounter Books, 2016.

Melcher, Mark L and Soukup, Stephen R. *Know Thine Enemy: A History of the Left.* Murrells Inlet: Covenant Books, Inc., 2018.

Millard, Catherine. *The Rewriting of America's History.* Camp Hill: Horizon House Publishers, 1991.

Orwell, George. *1984.* New York: Penguin Books, 1961.

Osterweil, Vicky. *In Defense of Looting: A Riotous History of Uncivil Action.* New York: PublicAffairs, 2020.

Sandefur, Timothy. *The Conscience of the Constitution: The Declaration of Independence and the Right of Liberty.* Washington DC: Cato Institute, 2014.

_____. *Frederick Douglass: Self-Made Man.* Washington DC: Cato Institute, 2018.

Schweikart, Larry. *A Patriot's History of the United States.* New York: Penguin Group, 2004.

Sowell, Thomas. *Intellectuals and Society.* New York: Basic Books, 2011.

Steele, Shelby. *The Content of Our Character: A New Vision of Race in America.* New York: Harper Perennial, 1998.

Ture, Kwame. *Black Power: The Politics of Liberation in America.* New York: Vintage Books, 1992.

Wayne Perryman. *Whites, Blacks and Racist Democrats: The Untold Story of Race & Politics within the Democratic Party from 1792–2009.* Bothwell: Book Publishers Network, 2010.

West, Cornel. *The Ethical Dimensions of Marxist Thought.* New York: Monthly Review Press, 1991.

Zinn, Howard. *A People's History of the United States.* New York: HarperCollins Publishers, 1999.

Articles

Abbott, Anna. "Howard Zinn's Fake History." *National Catholic Register*, May 16, 2020.

Adl-Tabatabai, Sean. "Marxist Angela Davis: BLM Riots are rehearsals for USA Revolution." *Daily Reformer*, August 29, 2020.

Anderson, Monica and Gustavo Lopez. "Key Facts about Black Immigrants to the U.S." January 24, 2018.

Basgen, Brian. "MIA: History: USA: The Black Panther Party." *Marxist Internet Archive*, 2002.

Beach, Kylie. "Shaun King Says White Jesus Statues Should Come Down." *Eternity News*, June 23, 2020.

Best, Ryan. "Confederate Statues Were Never Really About Preserving History." *FiveThirtyEight*, July 8, 2020.

BLM Staff. "Lessons from Fidel: Black Lives Matter and the Transition of El Comandante." *Black Lives Matter Global Network*, November 27, 2016.

Bradley, Anthony B. "The Marxist Roots of Black Liberation Theology." *Acton Institute*, April 2, 2008.

Brian. "'Cultural Purists' of the Progressive Persuasion: Cancel "Hamilton!" WIBC *Indy Mobile News*, June 30, 2020.

Brock, Jared. "The Story of Josiah Henson, the Real Inspiration for 'Uncle Tom's Cabin.'" *Smithsonian Magazine*, May 16, 2018.

Capehart, Jonathan. "'Hands Up, Don't Shoot' Was Built on a Lie." *The Washington Post*, March 16, 2015.

Dickstein, Corey. "Trump Promotes 100-Year-Old Tuskegee Airman to Brigadier General." *Stars and Stripes*, February 5, 2020.

Duara, Nigal. "Sanders, O'Malley Face Protestors at Netroots Nation Conference." *Los Angeles Times*, July 18, 2015.

Editorial Staff. "Black Lives Matter (BLM)." *DiscovertheNetworks*, September 12, 2020.

Editorial Staff, "Frederick Douglass: "The Meaning of July Fourth for the Negro." Zinn Education Project, October 5, 2005.

Editorial Staff. "Frederick Douglass—Blessing of Liberty and Education." *Teaching American History*, September 3, 1894.

Editorial Staff. "Learning from Harry Haywood in the Fight for Black Freedom and Socialism." *Fight Back! News*, August 13, 2020.

Editorial Staff. "Lincoln's Letter to Albert G. Hodges." *Teaching American History*, April 4, 1864.

Editorial Staff. "Origin of Freedom, Wisconsin." Wisconsin Historical Society, *Wausau Herald*, August 29, 1921.

Editorial Staff. "Police Shooting Database 2015–2020." *Washington Post*, September 10, 2020.

Editorial Staff. "Video: Frederick Douglass' Descendants Deliver His 'Fourth Of July' Speech." NPR, July 3, 2020.

Fryer, Roland G. "An Empirical Analysis of Racial Differences in Police Use of Force." Harvard University, 2016.

Gass, Nick. "'Hands Up, Don't Shoot' Ranked One of the Biggest 'Pinocchios' of 2015." *Politico*, December 14, 2015.

Gonzalez, Mike and Andrew Olivastro, "The Agenda of Black Lives Matter Is Far Different from the Slogan." *New York Post*, July 1, 2020.

Gonzalez, Pedro Blas. "Cultural Marxism, Antonio Gramsci, and the Frankfurt School." *Voegelin View*, March 31, 2018.

Grey, Barry. "Trump Gives Fascistic Rant at Mount Rushmore Event in Defiance of Health Experts." *World Socialist* Web Site, July 4, 2020.

Guelzo, Allen C. "'The 1619 Project' Tells a False Story About Capitalism, Too." *Wall Street Journal*, May 8, 2020.

Harris, Leslie M. "I Helped Fact-Check the 1619 Project. The Times Ignored Me." *Politico*, March 6, 2020.

Henry, Barbara. "Teaching Ruby Bridges." *The Boston Globe*, July 11, 2014.

Hill, Jason D. "My 'Black Lives Matter' Problem." *Commentary Magazine*, June 2018.

Jacobs, Jake. "The Twilight Zone of Marxist Angela Davis @ Lawrence University Today." *RenewAmerica*, January 20, 2016.

Johnson, Andre. Review of *Black Theology and Black Power* by James H. Cone. *Reading Religion*, July 31, 2019.

Johnson, David J. et al. "Officer Characteristics and Racial Disparities In Fatal Officer-Involved Shootings." *PNAS*, August 6, 2019.

Kass, John. "What Frightens the American Left: Larry Elder's New Documentary 'Uncle Tom.'" *Chicago Tribune*, July 1, 2020.

Kesler, Charles. "Call Them the 1619 Riots." *RealClearPolitics*, June 20, 2020.

Keyes, Allison. "The 'Clotilda,' the Last Known Slave Ship to Arrive in the U.S., Is Found." *Smithsonian Magazine*, May 22, 2019.

Kim, Wook. "The Top 10 Movie Dads We'd Use to Build the Perfect Father: Boyz n the Hood." *Time Magazine*, June 14, 2012.

Lindsay, James. "The Complex Relationship between Marxism and Wokeness." *New Discourses*, July 28, 2020.

_____. "Eight Big Reasons Critical Race Theory Is Terrible for Dealing with Racism." *New Discourses*, June 12, 2020.

Marini, John. "Frank Capra's America and Ours." *Imprimis*, March 2015.

Masnov, James M. "History Killers: The Academic Fraudulence of the 1619 Project." *New Discourses*, July 7, 2020.

Mendenhall, Allen. "Cultural Marxism Is Real" The James G. Martin Center for Academic Renewal, January 4, 2019.

Meyer, Joshua. "'Glory' at 30: Denzel Washington's 1989 Breakout Film Is Still the Best Civil War Movie Ever Made." *SlashFilm*, December 20, 2019.

Michals, Debra. "Ruby Bridges." National Women's History Museum, 2015.

Miller, Liam. "James Cone's Constructive Vision of Sin and the Black Lives Matter Movement." *Black Theology: An International Journal*, February 11, 2020.

Newman, Rena Yehuda. "Don't Mourn for Statues; Imagine What Can Flourish in Their Place." Madison.Com, July 1, 2020.

Ngugi, Mukoma Wa. "The Old-Time Religion of Cornel West's Marxism." *The Guardian*, June 4, 2011.

Phillips, Melanie. "Victim Culture Tears Up Jewish Moral Norms." *Israel Hayom*, June 5, 2020.

Pollak, Joel B. "Rioters Deface 'Glory' Monument to Black Civil War Soldiers in Boston." *American Priority*, June 2, 2020.

Reynolds, Barbara Ann. "I Was a Civil Rights Activist in the 1960s. But It's Hard for Me to Get Behind Black Lives Matter." *The Washington Post*, August 24, 2015.

Richardson, Valerie. "Larry Elder's Black Conservative Film Takes Top Spot for Documentaries." *The Washington Times*, July 20, 2020.

Schwartz, Ian. "Sen. Kaine: The United States Didn't Inherit Slavery, We Created It." *RealClearPolitics*, June 17, 2020.

Shenoy, Rupa. "'Willful Amnesia': How Africans Forgot—and Remembered—Their Role in the Slave Trade." *The World*, August 20, 2019.

Sieff, Kevin. "An African country Reckons with Its History of Selling Slaves." *Washington Post*, January 29, 2018.

Simpson, James. "Black Lives Matter: Racist Provocation with Radical Roots." *Capital Research Center*, September 21, 2016.

Strauss, Valerie. "Why an 1852 Speech by Frederick Douglass Should Be Taught to Students Today." *Washington Post*, July 4, 2019.

Thomas, Bradley. "Antonio Gramsci: The Godfather of Cultural Marxism." *FEE*, March 31, 2019.

Watson, John Henry. "What's Up with Francis and Communism?" *Choosing-Him* Catholic Blog, April 24, 2019.

Williams, Walter. "The True Plight of Black Americans." *The Northern Virginia Daily*, June 10, 2020.

Yumga, Nestride. "Violence Threatens Black Lives." *Wall Street Journal*, June 8, 2020.

Interviews

Ball, Jared. "A Short History of Black Lives Matter." The Real News Network, July 23, 2015.

Freeman, Morgan. "Freeman on Black History." *60 Minutes* with Mike Wallace. CBS News, December 18, 2005.

Levin, Mark. "Life and Liberty Interview with Bob Woodson." Fox News, July 6, 2020.

MacCallum, Martha. "The Story with Hawk Newsome." Fox News, June 25, 2020.

Rietz, Kristen. "The Town of Freedom and Black History Month." Central Wisconsin News, February 10, 2009.